EGGS EGGS EVERYWHERE

Teacher's Guide

Preschool–1

Skills

Observing, Comparing, Communicating, Organizing Data,
Role-Playing, Sorting, Classifying, Graphing, Logical Thinking

Concepts

Nesting and Parenting Behaviors, Habitat, Life Cycle, Sorting, Graphing,
Number Sense, Pattern Recognition, Form and Function,
Relationship of the Shape of an Object to Its Movement

Themes

Patterns of Change, Structure, Diversity and Unity

Mathematics Strands

Geometry, Logic and Language, Number, Pattern, Statistics

Nature of Science and Mathematics

Real-Life Applications, Interdisciplinary, Creativity and Constraints

by

Jean C. Echols
Kimi Hosoume
Jaine Kopp

LHS GEMS

GEMS
Great Explorations in Math and Science
Lawrence Hall of Science
University of California at Berkeley

Lawrence Hall of Science
    Chairman: Glenn T. Seaborg
    Director: Ian Carmichael

Initial support for the origination and publication of the GEMS series was provided by the A.W. Mellon Foundation and the Carnegie Corporation of New York. GEMS has received support from the McDonnell-Douglas Foundation and the McDonnell-Douglas Employees Community Fund, the Hewlett Packard Company Foundation, and the people at Chevron USA. GEMS gratefully acknowledges the contribution of word processing equipment from Apple Computer, Inc. This support does not imply responsibility for statements or views expressed in publications of the GEMS program.

Under a grant from the National Science Foundation, GEMS Leader's Workshops have been held across the country. For further information on GEMS leadership opportunities, or to receive a publication brochure and the *GEMS Network News*, please contact GEMS at the address and phone number provided.

Development of this guide was sponsored in part by the Department of Education Fund for the Improvement of Post-Secondary Education (FIPSE) and a grant from the National Science Foundation.

COMMENTS WELCOME

Great Explorations in Math and Science (GEMS) is an ongoing curriculum development project. GEMS guides are revised periodically, to incorporate teacher comments and new approaches. We welcome your criticisms, suggestions, helpful hints, and any anecdotes about your experience presenting GEMS activities. Your suggestions will be reviewed each time a GEMS guide is revised. Please send your comments to:

    University of California, Berkeley
    GEMS Revisions
    Lawrence Hall of Science # 5200
    Berkeley, CA 94720-5200

Our phone number is (510) 642-7771.
Our fax number is (510) 643-0309.

Great Explorations in Math and Science (GEMS) Program

The Lawrence Hall of Science (LHS) is a public science center of the University of California at Berkeley. LHS offers a full program of activities for the public, including workshops and classes, exhibits, films, lectures, and special events. LHS is also a center for teacher education and curriculum research and development.

Over the years, LHS staff developed a multitude of activities, assembly programs, classes, and interactive exhibits. These programs have proven successful at LHS and should be useful to schools, other science centers, museums, and community groups. A number of these guided-discovery activities are published under the Great Explorations in Math and Science (GEMS) title after an extensive refinement process that includes classroom testing, ensuring the use of easy-to-obtain materials, and carefully written step-by-step instructions and background information to allow presentation by teachers without special background in mathematics or science.

Contributing Authors

Jacqueline Barber
Katharine Barrett
Kevin Beals
Lincoln Bergman
Beverly Braxton
Kevin Cuff
Linda De Lucchi
Gigi Dornfest
Jean Echols
John Erickson
Philip Gonsalves
Jan M. Goodman
Alan Gould
Catherine Halversen
Kimi Hosoume
Sue Jagoda
Jaine Kopp
Linda Lipner
Larry Malone
Cary I. Sneider
Craig Strang
Debra Sutter
Jennifer Meux White
Carolyn Willard

ACKNOWLEDGMENTS

Photographs: Richard Hoyt
Cover: Lisa Haderlie Baker
Illustrations: Lisa Haderlie Baker, Rose Craig

Thanks to all the enthusiastic people at the Lawrence Hall of Science, including **Katharine Barrett, Beatrice Boffen,** and **Ellen Blinderman** for their suggestions and other contributions during the development and writing of *Eggs Eggs Everywhere.*

Thanks to **Ted Robertson** for his help in researching information for this guide and to the Associate Director for Education at U.C. Botanical Garden, Berkeley, **Jennifer Meux White,** for her scientific review of this guide.

Thanks to teachers **Maggie Swartz** and **Sally Barry** of Wilson Elementary in San Leandro, California, and **William Greene** of the Emeryville Child Development Center in Emeryville, California, for the generous gift of their time in allowing us to photograph the *Eggs Eggs Everywhere* activities in their classrooms. And, of course, thanks to all the children who enliven the photographs in this guide.

REVIEWERS

We would like to thank the following educators who reviewed, tested, or coordinated the reviewing of this series of GEMS/PEACHES materials in manuscript and draft form. Their critical comments and recommendations, based on presentation of these activities nationwide, contributed significantly to these GEMS publications. Their participation in the review process does not necessarily imply endorsement of the GEMS program or responsibility for statements or views expressed. Their role is an invaluable one, and their feedback is carefully recorded and integrated as appropriate into the publications.

ALASKA
Coordinator:
Cynthia Dolmas Curran

Creative Play Preschool, Wasilla
Ronda Ingham
Mary Percak-Dennett

Iditarod Elementary School, Wasilla
Beverly McPeek

Wasilla Middle School, Wasilla
Cynthia Dolmas Curran

CALIFORNIA
Coordinators: **Leslie Cooper, Karen Fong, Kathy Moran, Floria Spencer, Rebecca Wheat, Dottie Wiggins**

4C's Children's Center, Oakland
Yolanda Coleman-Wilson

24 Hour Children Center, Oakland
Sheryl Lambert
Ella Tassin
Inez Watson

Afterschool Program, Piedmont
Willy Chen

Alameda Head Start, Alameda
Michelle Garabedian
Debbie Garcia
Stephanie Josey

Albany Children's Center, Albany
Celestine Whittaker

Bancroft School, Berkeley
Cecilia Saffarian

Bartell Childcare and Learning Center, Oakland
Beverly Barrow
Barbara Terrell

Beach Elementary School, Piedmont
Ann Blasius
Juanita Forester
Elodee Lessley
Jean Martin

Belle Vista Child Development Center, Oakland
Satinder Jit K. Rana

Berkeley-Albany YMCA, Berkeley
Trinidad Caselis

Berkeley Hills Nursery School, Berkeley
Elizabeth Fulton

Berkeley/Richmond Jewish Community, Berkeley
Terry Amgott-Kwan

Berkeley Unified School District, Berkeley
Rebecca Wheat

Berkwood-Hedge School, Berkeley
Elizabeth Wilson

Bernice & Joe Play School, Oakland
Bernice Huisman-Humbert

Bing School, Stanford
Kate Ashbey

Brookfield Elementary School, Oakland
Kathy Hagerty
Linda Rogers

Brookfield Head Start, Oakland
Suzie Ashley

Butte Kiddie Corral, Shingletown
Cindy Stinar Black

Cedar Creek Montessori, Berkeley
Idalina Cruz
Jeanne Devin
Len Paterson

Centro Vida, Berkeley
Rosalia Wilkins

Chinese Community United Methodist Church, Oakland
Stella Ko Kwok

Clayton Valley Parent Preschool, Concord
Lee Ann Sanders
Patsy Sherman

Compañeros del Barrio State Preschool, San Francisco
Anastasia Decaristos
Laura Todd

Contra Costa College, San Pablo
Sylvia Alvarez-Mazzi

Creative Learning Center, Danville
Brooke H. B. D'Arezzo

Creative Play Center, Pleasant Hill
Debbie Coyle
Sharon Keane

Dena's Day Care, Oakland
Kawsar Elshinawy

Dover Preschool, Richmond
Alice J. Romero

Duck's Nest Preschool, Berkeley
Pierrette Allison
Patricia Foster
Mara Ellen Guckian
Ruth Major

East Bay Community Children's Center, Oakland
Charlotte Johnson
Oletha R. Wade

Ecole Bilingue, Berkeley
Nichelle R. Kitt
Richard Mermis
Martha Ann Reed

Emerson Child Development Center, Oakland
Ron Benbow
Faye McCurtis
Vicky Wills

Emerson Elementary School, Oakland
Pamela Curtis-Horton

Emeryville Child Development Center, Emeryville
Ellastine Blalock
Jonetta Bradford
William Greene
Ortencia A. Hoopii

Enrichment Plus Albert Chabot School, Oakland
Lisa Dobbs

Family Day Care, Oakland
Cheryl Birden
Penelope Brody
Eufemia Buena Byrd
Mary Waddington

Family Day Care, Orinda
Lucy Inouye

Gan Hillel Nursery School, Richmond
Denise Moyes-Schnur

Gan Shalom Preschool, Berkeley
Iris Greenbaum

Garner Toddler Center, Alameda
Uma Srinath

Gay Austin, Albany
Sallie Hanna-Rhyne

Giggles Family Day Care, Oakland
Doris Wührmann

Greater Richmond Social Services Corp., Richmond
Lucy Coleman

Happy Lion School, Pinole
Sharon Espinoza
Marilyn Klemm

Hintil Kuu Ca Child Development Center, Oakland
Eunice C. Blago
Kathy Moran
Gina Silber
Agnes Tso
Ed Willie

Jack-in-the-Box Junction Preschool, Richmond
Virginia Guadarrama

Kinder Care, Oakland
Terry Saugstad

King Child Development Center, Berkeley
Joan Carr
Diane Chan
Frances Stephens
Eula Webster
Dottie Wiggins

King Preschool, Richmond
Charlie M. Allums

The Lake School, Oakland
Margaret Engel
Patricia House
Vickie Stoller

Learning Adventures Child Development, Redding
Dena Keown

Longfellow Child Development Center, Oakland
Katryna Ray

Los Medanos Community College, Pittsburg
Judy Henry
Filomena Macedo

Maraya's Developmental Center, Oakland
Maria A. Johnson-Price
Gayla Lucero

Mark Twain School Migrant Education, Modesto
Grace Avila

Mary Jane's Preschool, Pleasant Hill
Theresa Borges

Merritt College Children's Center, Oakland
Deborah Green
Virginia Shelton

Mickelson's Child Care, Ramona
Levata Mickelson

Mills College Children's Center, Oakland
Monica Grycz

Mission Head Start, San Francisco
Pilar Marroquin
Mirna Torres

The Model School Comprehensive, Berkeley
Jenny Schwartz-Groody

Montclair Community Play Center, Oakland
Elaine Guttmann
Nancy Kliszewski
Mary Loeser

Next Best Thing, Oakland
Denise Hingle
Franny Minervini-Zick

Oak Center Christian Academy, Oakland
Debra Booze

Oakland Parent Child Center, Oakland
Barbara Jean Jackson

Oakland Unified School District, Oakland
Floria Spencer

Orinda Preschool, Orinda
Tracy Johansing-Spittler

Oxford St. Learning Road, Berkeley
Vanna Maria Kalofonos

Peixoto Children's Center, Hayward
Alma Arias
Irma Guzman
Paula Lawrence
Tyra Toney

Piedmont Cooperative Playschool, Piedmont
Marcia Nybakken

Playmates Daycare, Berkeley
Mary T. McCormick

Rainbow School, Oakland
Mary McCon
Rita Neely

San Antonio Head Start, Oakland
Cynthia Hammock
Ilda Terrazas

San Jose City College, San Jose
Mary Conroy

Sequoia Nursery School, Oakland
Karen Fong

Sequoyah Community Preschool, Oakland
Erin Smith
Kim Wilcox

Shakelford Head Start, Modesto
Teresa Avila

So Big Preschool, Antioch
Linda Kochly

St. Vincent's Day Home, Oakland
Pamela Meredith

Sunshine Preschool, Berkeley
Poppy Richie

U. C. Berkeley Child Care Services Smyth Fernwald II, Berkeley
Diane Wallace
Caroline W. Yee

Walnut Ave. Community Preschool, Walnut Creek
Evelyn DeLanis

Washington Child Development Center, Berkeley
Heather Jones

Washington Kids Club, Berkeley
Adwoa A. Mante
Westview Children's Center, Pacifica
Adrienne J. Schneider

Wilson Elementary, San Leandro
Sally Barry
Jason Browning
Maggie Swartz

Woodroe Woods, Hayward
Wendy Justice

Woodstock Child Development Center, Alameda
Mary Raabe
Denise M. Ratto

Woodstock School, Alameda
Amber D. Cupples

Yuk Yan Annex, Oakland
Eileen Lok

YWCA Oakland, Oakland
Iris Ezeb
Grace Perry

FLORIDA
Community Pre-School, Vero Beach
Joyce Parent
Peggy Stokes

Gulfstream Elementary, Miami
Channey Johnson

Osceola Magnet School, Vero Beach
Chris Dugan
Diane Egan
Carol Marino
Janet Meyer

MICHIGAN
Plymouth Canton Community School, Plymouth
Lisa Bouchillon
Karen Climer
Sally DeRoo
Colleen Jones
Debra Kava

MISSISSIPPI
Coordinator: **Josephine Gregory**

Little Village Child Development Center, Jackson
Josephine Gregory
Patrick Gregory
Denise Harris
Barbara Johnson

NEW JERSEY
South Mountain School, South Orange
Jayne Abrams
Jacqueline McGee
Nancy Pokotilow
Lisa Shifrin

NEW YORK
Coordinators: **Stephen Levey, Mary Jean Syrek**

Aquarium for Wildlife Conservation, Brooklyn
Meryl Kafka

Dr. Charles R. Drew Science Magnet, Buffalo
Linda Edwards
Carol Podger
Diana Roberts
Willie Robinson
Mary Jean Syrek

PS 329—Surfside School, Brooklyn
Sharon Fine
Valerie LaManna
Stephen Levey
Barbara Nappo
Angela Natale
Arline Reisman

TEXAS
Coordinator: **Myra Luciano**

Armand Bayou Elementary School, Houston
Myra Luciano
Peggy Niksich
Jeanne Vining

John F. Ward Elementary School, Houston
Brenad Greenshields
Luanne Lamar
Vicki Peterson
Jenny Scott

North Pointe Elementary School, Houston
Phyllis Berman

UTAH
Family Enrichment Center, Kaysville
Eileen Bernard
LouAnn Brough
Sunee Folkman
Sally Ogilvie

WASHINGTON
Coordinator: **Peggy Willcuts**

Blue Ridge Mountain School, Walla Walla
Elizabeth Arebalos
Sandi Burt
Gail Callahan
Leah Crudup
Peggy Willicuts

John Muir School, Seattle
Julie Frederick
Leanne Hust
Ann Kumata
Linda Mak
Cynthia Vice

CONTENTS

Introduction

The exploration of eggs is a fascinating way for young children to investigate the beginning of life of many animals. On the outside, eggs come in a variety of shapes, colors, and patterns. On the inside, a diversity of animals with feathers, scales, and slippery skin begin their lives in the small, confined space we call an egg. *Eggs Eggs Everywhere* introduces students to the wonder of eggs. Opportunities to read stories about eggs and the exciting animals inside are provided throughout the unit.

In **Activity 1**, the children begin their exploration of eggs by participating in The Chicken Drama, observing real chicken eggs, and role-playing chicks hatching out of eggs. The youngsters observe an assortment of real eggs and compare their size, shape, and color. Next, while playing with plastic eggs, the students discover a variety of toy animals—such as snakes, turtles, fish, and birds—inside the eggs and learn that these animals hatch from eggs.

In **Activity 2**, the students begin with Ruth Heller's beautifully illustrated book, *Chickens Aren't the Only Ones*, for a broad picture of the wealth of animals that hatch from eggs. The children open another plastic egg and find a plastic animal inside, which serves as a model of an animal that in real life hatches from an egg. Students then role-play the different animals that hatch from eggs.

Later in Activity 2, students again open a plastic egg and find an animal inside. The animals are organized and compared, using a large graphing grid, by the number of legs of each animal. As the students sort, classify, and graph, they use logical-thinking skills to organize data, use numbers in context, and make comparisons. Children also explore animals that lay their eggs on land and in water.

In **Activity 3**, the students get acquainted with a live box turtle by observing, touching, and feeding it. They learn more about turtles when they watch a drama about a mother turtle laying eggs and baby turtles crawling out of their underground nest. The students observe a live fish and learn what fish eat and how they move in water. They discover where fish lay their eggs. While watching the Baby Fish Drama the children learn that most newly hatched fish can take care of themselves as soon as they hatch from their eggs, that snakes slither on land and swim in water, and that some snakes eat fish.

The Literature Connections section on page 59 features many books we think will enhance this unit. At the end of each annotation we suggest the activity where the book makes a good connection.

In **Activity 4,** the final activity, the children freely explore the movement of plastic eggs and other objects on flat and inclined surfaces. They compare the movement of the eggs with a variety of objects they roll on the floor, into a box, and down a ramp. As the students investigate rolling objects, they gain elements of practical experience in physical science that prepare them for later learning.

The students then participate in a drama about a murre, a seabird that lays its egg on a narrow cliff above the ocean. The children discover that the shape of the murre's egg enables it to roll in a small circle—and not off the cliff. The students explore objects that roll in a circle and role-play seabirds on a cliff with their eggs. This final activity helps the students understand that shapes in nature often serve an important function.

The variety of life that hatches from eggs, and the ingeniousness of nature in the myriad shapes and forms of eggs, opens up to young children the wonders of the natural world. The exciting exploration of eggs encompasses concepts in biology, physical science, and mathematics that will provide a valuable and essential groundwork as they continue to explore nature.

GEMS and PEACHES

GEMS is publishing a number of early childhood activity guides developed by the PEACHES project of the Lawrence Hall of Science. PEACHES is a curriculum development and training program for teachers and parents of children in preschool through first grade.

Like the GEMS guides already available for preschool and the early grades—such as *Hide A Butterfly*, *Animal Defenses*, and *Buzzing A Hive*—the PEACHES guides combine free exploration, drama, art, and literature with science and mathematics to give young children positive and effective learning experiences.

Activity 1: Exploring Eggs

Overview

Many animals, from a tiny insect to a huge turtle, hatch from an egg to start their lives. The children begin their exploration of eggs by participating in The Chicken Drama, observing real chicken eggs, and role-playing chicks hatching out of eggs. In Session 2, the youngsters observe an assortment of real eggs and compare their size, shape, and color. Next, while playing with plastic eggs, the students discover a variety of toy animals—such as snakes, turtles, fish, and birds—inside the eggs and learn that these animals hatch from eggs. While looking at posters and pictures of animal nests, the youngsters discover several habitats where animals lay their eggs.

Session 1: What is an Egg?

What You Need

For the group

❑ 1 container, such as a bowl or basket, large enough to hold a chicken egg for each child

❑ Pictures of chickens hatching from eggs (see Resources on page 56 for books with pictures you can use)

optional

   ❑ 1 live chicken

For each child

❑ 1 real chicken egg (hard-boiled)

For the drama

❑ 1 girl doll

❑ Enough dry grass or straw to make a nest 8" to 12" in diameter

❑ 1 Chicken and Her Eggs poster (see page 12)

optional

   ❑ 1 toy chicken

Getting Ready

Anytime Before the Activity

Hard boil the chicken eggs.

Immediately Before the Activity

Place the chicken eggs in the bowl to distribute later.

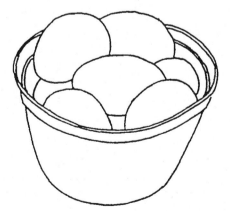

Setting Up for The Chicken Drama

1. Shape the straw into a nest (about 8" to 12" in diameter) and place the nest on the floor in the area where you plan to present The Chicken Drama.

2. Place one egg in the nest. Have two other eggs available to add to the nest as you tell the story.

3. Have the doll nearby.

The Chicken Drama

1. Gather the children in a circle on the floor and ask, "What is an egg?" Allow time for the youngsters to express their ideas and then ask,
   "Who has seen a real egg?"
   "What kind of egg was it?"
   "Where did you see it?"

2. Present a short drama to introduce the topic of eggs. Use three chicken eggs, the nest, and the doll to dramatize the following story.
   • A little girl named Linda lives on a farm. Each morning she gets up early and goes to the barn to milk her goat. (Move the doll over to the nest.)
   • Look what she sees!
     (Bend the doll over as though she is peering into the nest. Have her turn to the class and ask, "What is it?") [an egg]
   • That night Linda goes to sleep.
     (Lay the doll down on the floor. Tell the students to close their eyes and pretend they are sleeping. Put a second egg in the nest.)

- Early the next morning Linda goes to the barn to milk her goat. Look what she finds!
- How many eggs do you see? [two]
- That night Linda goes to sleep. (Lay the doll down on the floor. Tell the children to close their eyes and pretend they are sleeping. Put a third egg in the nest.)
- Early the next morning Linda goes to the barn to milk her goat. Look what she finds!
- How many eggs do you see now? [three]
  (Ask, "What animal do you think laid these eggs?" Allow time for the students to take turns guessing.)

3. Show the class the Chicken and Her Nest poster and a toy chicken, if you have one.

4. Ask, "What do you think Linda could do with the eggs?" Tell the group some chicken eggs are eaten and some chicken eggs hatch into baby chicks.

5. Ask questions that encourage the youngsters to talk about their experiences with live chickens.
   "Have you ever seen a live chicken?"
   "Where did you see it?"
   "What was it doing?"
optional
   Let the children see and touch a real chicken.

Observing Chicken Eggs

1. Give a chicken egg in a container to each child and ask,
   "What kind of egg is this?"

2. Ask questions to encourage the students to observe and feel the eggs.
   "What color is your egg?"
   "How does it feel?"
   "Do you see cracks in it?"
   "Do you see any spots on it?"
   "What else do you see on your egg?"

3. Collect the eggs and container.

Role-playing

1. Role-play with the students the drama of chicks hatching out of eggs.
   - Curl up as small as possible and pretend you are inside an eggshell.
   - Wiggle inside your eggshell.
   - Use your beak (face) to poke holes in your eggshell.
   - Make cracking sounds as you break through your eggshell.
   - Shake off your feathers and walk away on wobbly legs.

2. Show the students pictures of newly hatched chicks.

Creative Play

Let the children play with the doll, toy chicken, nest, and eggs.

Going Further

1. Let the students eat the hard-boiled eggs or use them to make egg salad. They could also use raw eggs in a cooking activity.

2. Invite children to share their egg traditions with the class. (See *Renchenka's Eggs* in the Literature Connections on page 61 and the resource book, *Decorative Eggs*, on page 56, as well as additional information on the cultural connections to eggs on page 52.)

Session 2: A Variety of Eggs and Animals

What You Need

For the group

❑ 1 container, such as a basket

❑ A variety of real eggs, such as frog, duck, quail, silk moth, and snail—aquatic or garden. (See Resources on page 57 for supply houses that sell prepared real eggs, such as ostrich eggs.)

❑ 1 Snake Laying Eggs poster (see page 13)

❑ 1 Robin and Her Nest poster (see page 14)

❑ 1 Ostrich and Her Eggs poster (see page 15)

❑ Pictures of animals hatching from eggs or laying eggs (see Resources on page 56 for books with pictures you can use)

For each child and yourself

❑ 1 hollow plastic egg that opens and closes—include a few extra eggs in case some break (Many variety, grocery, and drug stores sell plastic eggs before Easter. You will use these plastic eggs again in Activity 2, Session 2.)

❑ 1 small toy animal that hatches from an egg—and can fit inside a plastic egg—such as a turtle, lizard, spider, snake, bird, or fish (Include a few extra toy animals in case some get lost. You will use these toy animals again in Activity 2, Session 2.)

Duck and quail eggs are often found in specialty grocery stores and are easily "blown out" for display.

__To blow out a raw egg (remove the insides)__ poke a small hole in each end and blow steadily through one end. The yolk and white will flow out through the second hole. If you decide to buy fertile eggs and incubate them, see page 58 for information on incubators.

Getting Ready

Several Days or Weeks Before the Activity

1. Find a variety of real eggs. Although it takes time and effort to collect them, the benefits to the children are worth it. Seeing, comparing, and holding real eggs ties this whole unit to the natural world, and deepens the learning.

2. You may want to enlarge the posters to 11" x 17" for easier viewing.

Immediately Before the Activity

1. Put the toy animals inside the plastic eggs.

2. Place the eggs in the play area, preferably outside, where the girls and boys can find them easily.

3. Gather the real eggs together in one place for the students to observe.

Observing a Variety of Real Eggs

1. Have the children observe, in your room or in nature, live or preserved eggs such as quail, duck, frog, ant, silk moth, and snail (aquatic or garden).

2. In small groups, encourage the boys and girls to compare and discuss the size, shape, and color of the eggs. As they focus on size, challenge the children to place the eggs in size order from smallest to largest.

If you remove eggs from nature, be responsible about which eggs you take. If the young, such as birds, are dependent on their parents, don't take the eggs from the nest. Snail and insect eggs can be brought into the classroom. After the students have observed the eggs (or the young if they hatch), return them to their natural habitat. Collecting eggs is prohibited in some areas, such as in parks, reserves, preserves, and National Seashores. Remember the saying, "take only photographs, leave only footprints."

Animal Pictures

1. Show the Snake Laying Eggs poster to the group. Ask,
   "What do you see in this picture?"
   "Where is the mother snake laying her eggs?" [on the ground]

2. Display the Robin and Her Nest poster and ask,
   "What do you see in this picture?"
   "Where did the robin make her nest?" [in a tree]
   "How many eggs do you see in the nest?
   "What do you think the robin used to make her nest?"

3. Show the Ostrich and Her Eggs poster and ask,
   "What do you see in this picture?"
   "Where did the ostrich lay her eggs?" [on the ground]
   "How many eggs do you see?"
   "How many chicks do you see?"

4. Show pictures of other animals hatching from eggs or laying eggs.

Find an Egg

1. Show the children a plastic egg and tell them they are going to look for eggs shaped like the plastic egg.

2. Take the group to the play area, and tell each child to find one egg to take back to the circle.

3. Back at the circle, encourage the youngsters to shake the eggs gently and listen to the sound.

4. Have the boys and girls open their eggs and take turns identifying the animals inside. Tell the group that real birds, fish, turtles, snakes, spiders, and lizards (name the toy animals you have) hatch from eggs.

5. Have the children put the animals back inside the eggs and collect the eggs in the basket.

6. Tell the students they will have time later to play with the animals and the eggs.

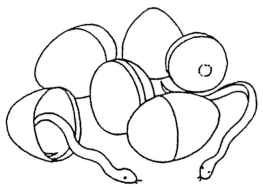

Egg Play

1. Leave the basket of plastic eggs and toy animals in an area where small groups of children can play freely with them.

2. Have the students guess what is inside the closed eggs by gently shaking and listening to the egg. They can open them to find out.

3. When the students finish playing, ask them to put the animals back inside the eggs, close the eggs, and put the eggs back in the basket.

Some K–1 teachers move directly to Activity 2 at this point.

Going Further

1. Incubating chicken, quail, or duck eggs in the classroom is a wonderful experience for students. Before deciding to do this, make arrangements for a future home for the birds that hatch. A local farm, a pet store, or a 4-H club may adopt them. Remember, never release them into the wild. You will need fertile eggs and an incubator. For information about purchasing eggs and an incubator, see Resources on page 58. Instructions on how to incubate the eggs usually come with the incubator.

2. Silkworm larvae are easy to rear from eggs in the spring. The students delight in handling the silkworms and taking turns feeding them. You will need a continuous supply of mulberry leaves for them to eat as that is the only food they eat.

3. Bring live animals that hatch from eggs, such as snakes, lizards, and birds, into the classroom for the children to see and hold.

4. Plan a field trip to a nature center, zoo, or science museum where the children can see a variety of animals that hatch from eggs.

Chicken and Her Eggs

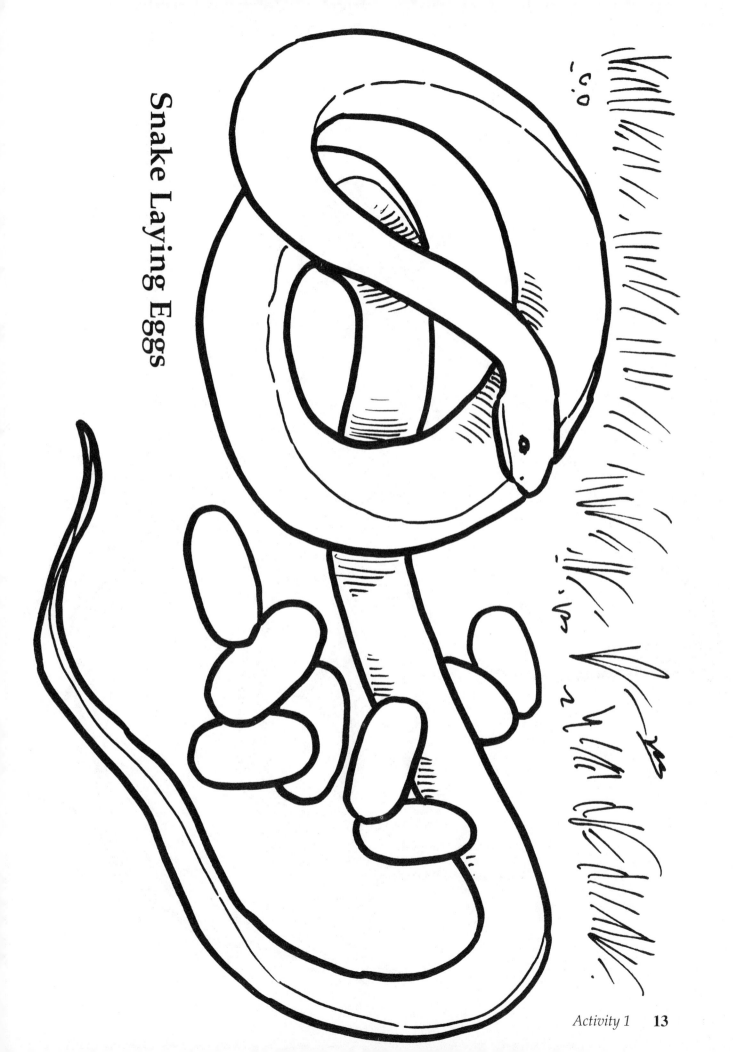

Snake Laying Eggs

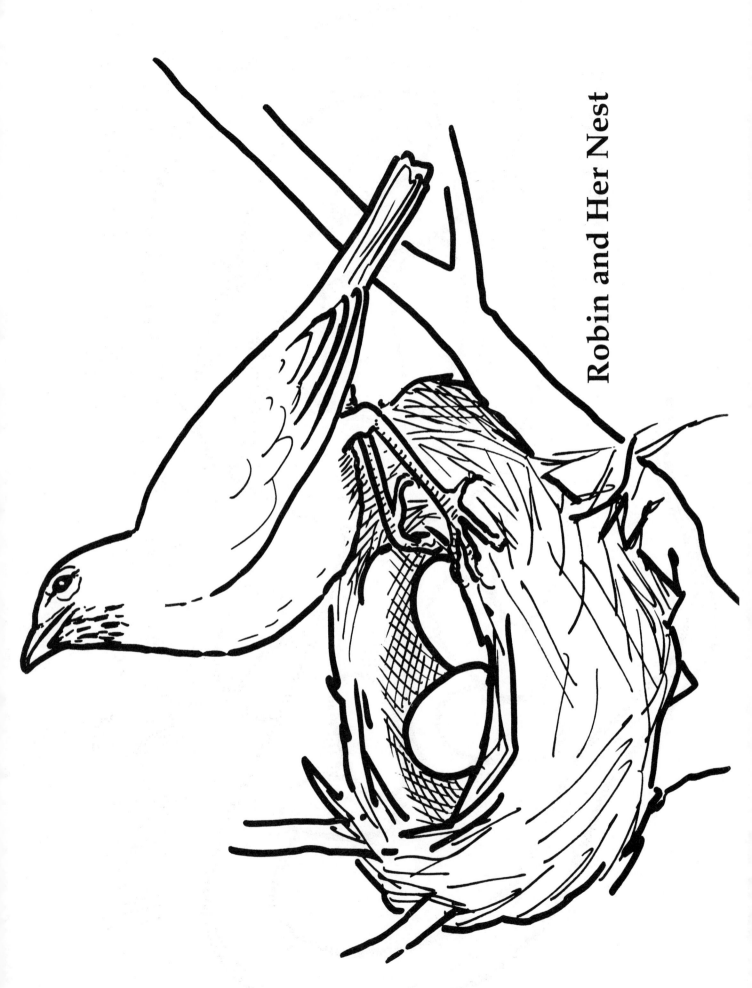

Robin and Her Nest

Ostrich and Her Eggs

Activity 2: Hatching Eggs

The students are given an idea of the multitude of animals that hatch from eggs—starting with a reading of Ruth Heller's beautifully illustrated book, *Chickens Aren't the Only Ones*. They open more plastic eggs and find toy animals inside. The plastic animals represent animals that in real life hatch from eggs, and are used for sorting, classifying, and graphing activities.

In **Session 1**, the students open their eggs and identify the animals inside. The toy animals are sorted by type. After the animals are sorted, the children count the number in each group and compare the quantities of each type of animal. As an active finale to this session, children role-play the different animals that hatch from eggs.

In **Session 2**, students again open a plastic egg and find an animal inside. The animals are organized and compared, using a large graphing grid, by looking at the number of legs on each animal. Using a two-bar graph, the number of animals with legs is compared to the number of animals without legs. For children with previous graphing experience, you may want to graph those same animals again, organizing them by how many legs there are on each animal.

As the students sort, classify, and graph, they focus on the physical characteristics of an animal (legs or no legs, how many legs), and use logical-thinking skills to organize data. As they analyze the data, they make comparisons and use numbers in a meaningful context.

Session 1: Sorting Animals

What You Need
For the class
- ❏ 1 copy of *Chickens Aren't the Only Ones* by Ruth Heller (See Literature Connections on page 59.)
- ❏ 1 basket or container to hold the filled plastic eggs (used in Activity 1)
- ❏ 6" white paper plates

For each child and yourself
- ❏ 1 hollow plastic egg that opens and closes (include a few extra eggs in case some break)
- ❏ 1 small toy animal that hatches from an egg, such as a turtle, lizard, spider, snake, bird, or fish

optional
- ❏ Ostrich Egg drawing (see page 28)
- ❏ Drawing of various eggs (see page 29)
- ❏ Crayons or markers
- ❏ Scissors

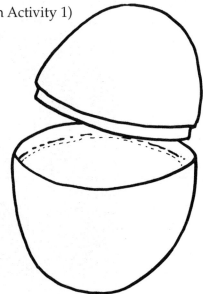

Getting Ready
Immediately Before the Activity

When you put an animal inside each egg, choose a variety of animals so the children will have a sense of the large number of animals in nature that hatch from eggs.

1. Put one toy animal inside each plastic egg. Put the filled eggs in a basket or container.

2. Set aside an egg with a fish in it for yourself.

3. Gather the paper plates. You need the same number of plates as types of animals that are in the eggs. For example, if you have fish, turtles, lizards, spiders, snakes, birds, and crickets, you will need seven plates.

optional

Decide if you want to do any of the Going Further activities (page 20) that involve coloring and cutting out a variety of egg models. For preschoolers, the Ostrich Egg drawing on page 28 is most appropriate. For older students, use the sheet depicting a variety of eggs on page 29. Duplicate enough copies so that each child has a sheet.

Animal Sorting

1. Gather the students in the group area of your room. Ask them what animals hatch from eggs.

2. Read *Chickens Aren't the Only Ones* to your class. If it is not available, read another book about animals hatching from eggs or show pictures of different animal eggs. Discuss the variety of animals that hatch from eggs. (Literature Connections on page 59 and Resources on page 56 list additional good books.)

3. Hold up your plastic egg. Ask the children what might be inside. Shake the egg. Is there a sound? Tell the children to guess what animal might hatch from it. Say something such as, "Tap, tap the egg cracked" and then open the egg. Be sure everyone sees the fish that "hatched" from the egg.

4. Tell the students they will each get a plastic egg with an animal inside. Distribute the eggs. When each child has an egg, they can shake it and guess what animal is inside. They can tell their guesses to each other as they wait for everyone to get an egg.

5. After everyone has one egg, have everyone say, "Tap, tap, the egg cracked," and have everyone open their eggs together! As the children delight in the animals, collect the plastic eggshells in the basket.

6. Have the students place their animals in front of them so everybody can see all the animals.

7. Place one paper plate in the center of the group. Hold up your fish and ask how fish move. Have your fish "swim" to the plate. Ask if there are other fish. Have those fish swim to the plate as well. Ask, "How many fish are on the plate now?"

8. Place a second paper plate in the center of the group. Ask who found a different kind of animal in the egg. If a child says he found a spider, ask how spiders move. Have all the spiders "crawl" or "climb" onto the next paper plate.

9. Continue by placing another plate in the center. Ask if anyone found a lizard. How do lizards move? Have the lizards "scurry" or "run" onto the plate.

10. Ask questions about other groups of animals. Each time a new animal is named, have that type of animal move in an appropriate way—creep or crawl or walk or slide—onto a plate.

11. When all the animals are on the plates, review the names of the animals. Count the number of animals on each plate. After you count all the groups, ask questions that focus on the number of animals on each plate.
    "Which plates have only two animals?"
    "How many plates have more than three animals?"
    "Which plate has the most animals?"
    "Which plate has the fewest number of animals?"

    For older children, you may want to ask additional questions that involve combining groups.
    "If you put the snakes and the fish together, how many animals would you have?"
    "If you put all the plates with just two animals together, how many animals would you have?" (This is a nice opportunity to count by both 1's and 2's.)
    "How many animals are there altogether?"

12. Ask what all the animals have in common. [they all hatch from eggs] Tell the students the eggs and animals will be available for them to explore later.

Role-playing Animals

1. Conclude the section with an egg-hatching drama.
    a. Have the students find their own special places in an area you designate.
    b. Review aloud the animals they just sorted.
    c. Have them silently choose to be one of the animals that hatches from an egg.
    d. Tell them to curl up as small as possible and pretend they are inside an egg.
    e. Guide them through the hatching process. For example, say they are growing bigger and bigger inside their eggs. Have them wiggle around inside their eggshells. Next, have them poke holes in their shells. Finally, have them hatch out of the eggs.
    f. Have them return to the group area by role-playing the movements of the animals they are pretending to be.

2. When the students are gathered in the group area, encourage them to continue role-playing in a guessing game. Let a volunteer role-play the movement of an animal while the rest of the children guess which animal the child is imitating.

Going Further
Decorating Eggs

Give each child a paper egg to decorate. You may want to choose an egg that is a different than a hen's egg—such as a turtle egg, which is round, or a snake egg, which is elliptical, or an ostrich egg, which is the largest egg laid. Have the students sort the eggs according to how they are decorated.

For Kindergarten and First Grade
1. Coloring Eggs

Make a copy of the sheet with the egg drawings (see page 29) for each child, or make your own sheet with egg drawings. Be sure to include a drawing of any real egg the students observed firsthand. Vary the drawings of eggs by shape and size such as a turtle egg (round), a fish egg (small, round), a hen egg (ovoid), a robin egg (small ovoid), a snake egg (elliptical), or an ostrich egg (largest egg laid). Have the students color the eggs. You may want to encourage them to copy the natural coloration. They can cut out the eggs and sort and classify them in different ways.

2. "Find My Egg" Bulletin Board

Make a large one-dimensional paper basket out of construction or butcher/chart paper that can hold all the children's eggs, and which you can mount on a bulletin board. Have each child contribute one decorated egg to this basket. The children can write or dictate a description of their eggs on small cards or egg-shaped sheets of paper. The students can have fun guessing each other's eggs using the descriptions.

3. Class Book on Eggs

To make a class book, have each child paste a decorated egg on a sheet of paper and dictate or write a sentence to describe it. Decorate the cover of the book with small eggs colored by the students. You may even want to make the book in the shape of an egg!

4. Egg-Hatching Cards

Cut a sheet of paper in half lengthwise to make sheets that are 4½" x 11". Holding the paper the long way, fold it a third of the way down from the top. Have the children draw an egg shape on the card and write "What's Hatching?" on the top half of the egg. Next, have the children lift the flap and draw a picture of an animal hatching from the egg. They can also write the name of the animal. These cards can be put up on a bulletin board.

Session 2: Organizing Sorts Into Graphs
For Kindergarten and First Grade ONLY!

What You Need

For the class
- ❏ 1 two-sided graphing grid (To make this you need butcher/chart paper, a permanent black marker, and a yardstick.)
- ❏ Labels (3" x 3" Post-Its or paper squares)
- ❏ 2 small trays or two 9" white paper plates
- ❏ 1 basket or container to hold the filled plastic eggs (used in Session 1)

For each child and yourself
- ❏ 1 hollow plastic egg that opens and closes—include a few extra eggs in case some break (You can use the same ones from Activity 1, Session 2.)
- ❏ 1 small toy animal that hatches from an egg, such as a turtle, lizard, spider, snake, bird, or fish (You can use the same ones from Activity 1, Session 2.)

Getting Ready

Anytime Before the Activity

1. Make a graphing grid. You will only need to make this once and can use it for many math and science activities.

    This graphing grid has two sides: Side 1 has two rows and 16 columns of boxes—this is used to graph the animals with legs and animals without legs; Side 2 has six rows and 16 columns—this is used to graph the animals by the number of legs.

 Side 1

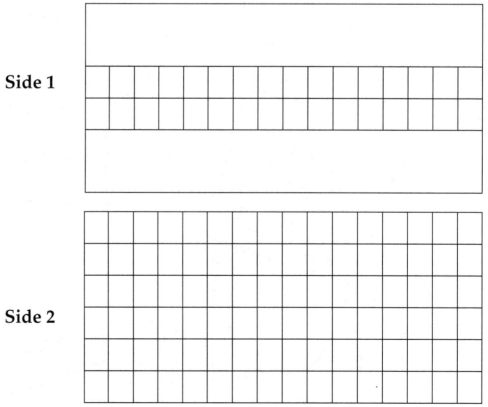

Side 2

To make the graph:
a. Cut a sheet of butcher/chart paper 24" wide by 64" long.
b. The next steps involve a series of folds to create the grid.
   1) Fold the paper in half lengthwise to measure 12" x 64". Crease the fold line.
   2) Fold this long piece into thirds. Do not worry about being perfect. It will measure 4" x 64". Crease the fold lines.
   3) Open up the paper to its full size. There will be five crease lines that are the length of the paper.
   4) Fold the paper in half to measure 24" x 32". Crease the fold line.
   5) Fold the paper in half again to measure 24" x 16". Crease the fold line.
   6) Continue to fold the paper in half and crease each fold until the paper measures 24" x 4".
   7) Open up the paper to its full size. A 4" x 4" grid is created by the crease lines, which will be marked.

c. On one side of the paper, create the two-row, 16-column graphing grid in the **center** of the paper. With the permanent black marker and yardstick, draw a line along the center crease line that divides the paper in half lengthwise. Then draw a line on the two crease lines above and below the center line. There are now three parallel lines. Complete the grid by drawing perpendicular lines to make 4-inch boxes. The finished grid for Side 1 will be two boxes deep and 16 boxes long.

d. On the reverse side (Side 2), create the large graphing grid. With the permanent black marker and yardstick, draw lines along all the crease lines to create a grid six boxes by 16 boxes.

3. Make labels for the number-of-legs graphing activity. Use either 3" x 3" Post-Its or 3" x 3" pieces of paper. Write the numbers 0, 2, 4, 6, 8, 10 in large letters on the paper you use, one number per paper. (We recommend doing the numbers in this way—rather than writing them permanently on the grid—so the grid remains flexible and can be used for other graphing activities.)

optional
   Laminate the grid for greater durability.

Immediately Before the Activity
1. Make your selection of plastic animals to fill the eggs.
   Select your animals depending on the graphing you want to do. If you are **only** sorting and graphing by legs and no legs, be sure that there is more of one type than the other, but not too many more. Some students may be ready to do a second graph sorting the same animals by the *number* of legs.

   If you plan to graph the animals a second time, be sure that there is a distribution of animals with 0, 2, 4, 6, 8, and 10 legs. It does not matter if in the first graph there are more animals with legs than without legs. It is also fine if you do not have animals in every category.

Here is a list of animals to assist you in making a selection.

If you have difficulty finding grasshoppers and crickets—which do not go through a complete metamorphosis—use ants, flies, or other more readily available insects. Those insects emerge from eggs as worm-like larva and don't develop their legs until later.

No Legs
- fish (including sea horses)
- snakes
- slugs or snails

2 Legs
- birds
- pteranadon or pterodactyl (prehistoric flying reptiles)

4 Legs
- turtles
- lizards
- dinosaurs (those that stand on four legs)

6 Legs
- grasshoppers, crickets

8 Legs
- spiders
- scorpions
- octopuses

10 Legs
- crabs (crabs and lobsters have eight "regular" legs and two "modified legs," which are claws)
- lobsters

2. Put the toy animals inside the plastic eggs. Place the eggs in a basket.

3. Gather two paper plates or trays and the graphing grid.

4. If you are doing the second graph, gather the number labels for the graph.

Animal Sorting and Graphing

1. Gather the children in a circle in the group area of your room. Tell them they will crack open another plastic egg. Review the guidelines for opening eggs as described in Session 1.

2. Distribute the eggs. Have the students predict what animal is inside. When everyone has an egg, together say, "tap, tap, the egg cracked!" As students open their eggs and examine their animals, collect the plastic eggshells.

3. Ask the students to check to see if their animals have legs or not.

4. Tell the children they are going to sort their animals into two groups: "Animals with Legs" and "Animals Without Legs." Show them the two paper plates where they will put their animals. Place the plates on the floor so all the children can see them.

5. Ask if anyone opened an egg that had an animal **without** legs. Choose a volunteer to identify and show his animal without legs to the group. Guide him to the appropriate plate to place his animal.

6. Ask if anyone opened an egg that had an animal **with** legs. Choose a volunteer to identify and show her animal with legs to the group. Guide her to the appropriate plate to place her animal.

7. Now that the two categories have been established, have each child in turn place their animal on the appropriate plate.

8. When all the animals are placed, have the students predict which is the largest group of animals—those with legs or those without legs. Ask how they can determine with certainty which group has more. [counting]

9. Introduce the students to the graphing grid.
   a. Place the graph (side 1) in the center of the group area.
   b. Tell the students you are going to put the animals on the graphing grid according to how they were sorted.
   c. Start at one end of the graph and place an animal without legs in one of the boxes. Place an animal with legs in the box next to the animal without legs.

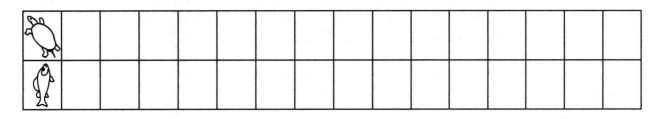

   d. Tell the students you are going to place all the animals on the graph with their help.
   e. Hold up an animal. Ask if it has legs or not. Place it in appropriate row. Hold up another animal. Ask where it belongs. Place it appropriately.
   f. Continue in a similar fashion until all the animals are placed. You may want to enlist the assistance of the children in actually placing the animals on the graph.

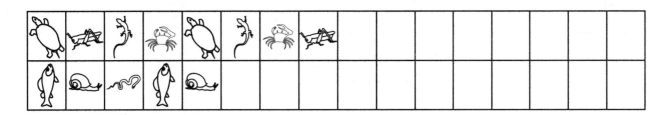

10. Ask the children again which group has more animals—those with legs or those without legs. Have them tell by looking at the graph. Explain this is one of the reasons for using a graph—to help organize information.

11. Count the number of animals in each row. Ask how many more animals with legs are on the graph than without legs (or vice versa). Demonstrate how to count extra animals in the row that has the most animals.
    a. Start at the beginning of the graph where the first animals were placed.
    b. Point out there is an animal with legs next to an animal without legs. Have the students think of these two as "partners."
    c. Go to the next two "partners" on the graph. Ask the children if each animal has a partner.
    d. With the children, keep giving each animal a partner until there is a column that has animals without partners.

e. Count the number of animals without partners. That is how many more animals there are (either with legs or without legs). In the graph on page 25, there are three more animals with legs than without legs.

Graph Again!

1. While the graph is still in place, tell the children you want to organize the animals by the number of legs on each animal.

2. Gather the animals and give each child one animal. Have them count the legs on their animals.

3. Have labels for the graph with the number 0, 2, 4, 6, 8, and 10 written on them. Turn the graph to Side 2 with six rows and 16 columns. Place the numbers in the first box at one end of the graph.

10															
8															
6															
4															
2															
0															

4. Ask for an animal with no legs. Place that animal in the row with the "0." Next, ask for an animal with two legs. Place it in the row labeled "2."

5. Continue until all the numbers in the rows have an animal with the corresponding number of legs.

6. Once the graph is started in this manner, have each child, one at a time, place their animal in the appropriate box on the graphing grid.

7. Ask questions related to the data on the graph.
   "How many animals on the graph have __ legs?" (0/2/4/6/8/10)
   "Are there more animals with ___ legs or ___ legs?"
   "How many more animals have ___ legs than ___legs?"

For students in first grade, you may also want to ask questions using the concept of **fewer than**.

"Are there fewer animals with ___ legs than ___ legs?"

"How many fewer animals have ___ legs than ___ legs?"

You may also want to ask questions that give children practice in adding numbers.

"If we added the number of animals with two legs and the number of animals with eight legs together, how many animals would we have?"

8. Remind the children what all the animals have in common—they all hatch from eggs.

In the GEMS guide Sifting Through Science, *a two-column graph is used to organize results of sink/ float and magnetism investigations.*

For kindergarten and older students, the GEMS Treasure Boxes *guide has ideas for graphing collections of "treasures" such as rocks, stamps, bread tags, pasta, and seeds.*

Going Further

More Two-Column Graphing

Create more two-column graphs using the graphing grid. Graph the plastic animals that fly with those that do not, or graph the animals that only live in the water with those that do not. For the children who have a snack daily, you can graph their preferences between two choices, such as a carrot or celery stick, apple or orange slice, square or round cracker, a pretzel stick or twist. Other two-column graphs could include whole and broken crayons, things in the room that are round and not round, and bottle caps with pictures and those without pictures.

Graph On!

Using the grid with six rows, you can extend the type of graphs you do to include 3-, 4-, 5-, and 6-row graphs by increasing the number of snack choices. You could also graph a collection of buttons by the number of holes. Graph the color preferences of your students using a rainbow of up to six colors or up to six shades of a particular color (for example, light pink to dark magenta). Your children can be great resources for ideas for new graphs.

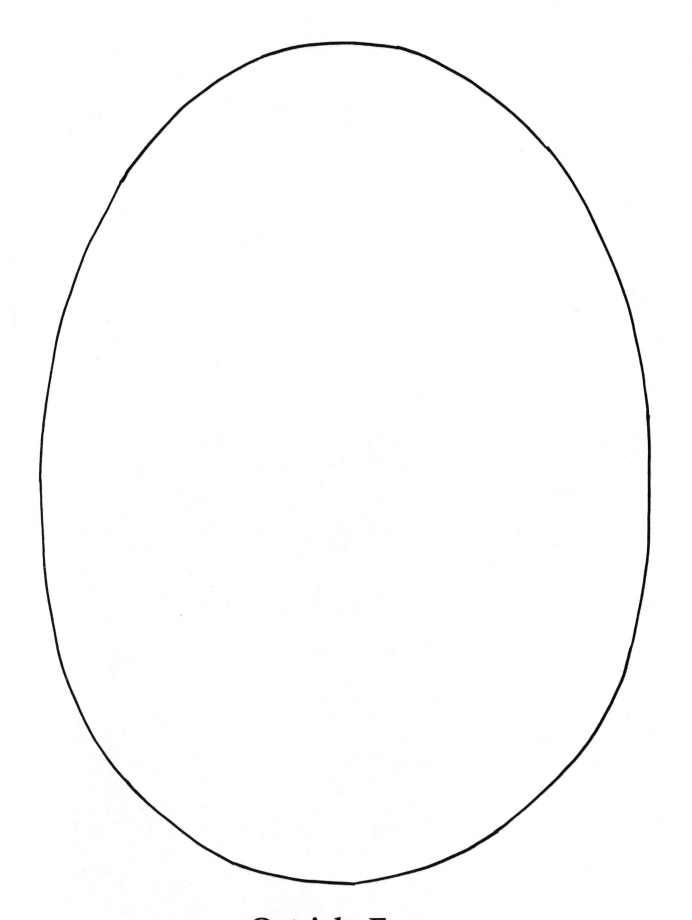

Ostrich Egg

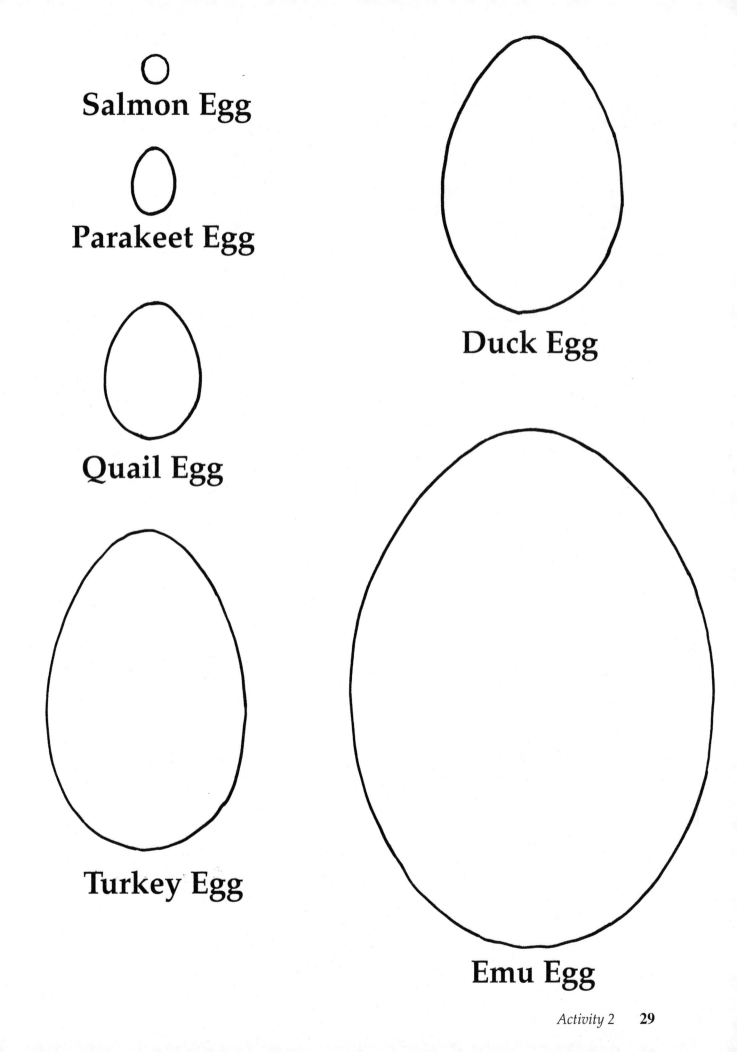

Salmon Egg

Parakeet Egg

Quail Egg

Turkey Egg

Duck Egg

Emu Egg

Activity 3: Eggs on Land, Eggs in Water

Overview

Animals lay eggs in many different places, including in water, on the ground, on leaves, and underground. In Session 1: Eggs on Land, the youngsters get to know a live box turtle by observing, touching, and feeding it. They learn more about turtles through a drama about a mother turtle laying eggs and baby turtles crawling out of their underground nest.

In Session 2: Eggs in Water, the students observe a live fish and learn what fish eat and how they move in water. While looking at a poster, they discover where fish lay their eggs.

In the Baby Fish Drama, the students learn that most newly hatched fish can take care of themselves as soon as they hatch from their eggs. They discover that baby fish not only eat pond plants but they also hide in them, that snakes slither on land and swim in water, and that some snakes eat fish.

At the end of the activity, the children are encouraged to play with plastic eggs and toy animals in tubs filled with water and tubs filled with sand. While playing with these materials, the students create their own dramas that recall the ideas presented.

Session 1: Eggs on Land

Box turtles are a common classroom pet and hopefully you can borrow one from another classroom, a nature center, or a student's home. Pet stores often carry box turtles but we recommend borrowing one for these activities as it is a large commitment to properly care for one. See page 32 for how to care for a box turtle.

What You Need
For the whole group
- ❏ 1 live box turtle
- ❏ 1 large toy turtle
- ❏ 2 small toy turtles
- ❏ 2 ping-pong balls or Styrofoam balls (as turtle eggs)
- ❏ 1 toy dog
- ❏ 1 tub, such as a dishpan, filled with sand
- ❏ 1 paper grocery bag
- ❏ 1 Turtle Laying Eggs poster (see page 38)
- ❏ Colored pictures of turtles and turtle eggs (See Resources on pages 58 for books with pictures you can use.)
- ❏ 2 strawberries
- ❏ 1 tomato, cut into quarters

optional

You can use a piece of clay to make the two small turtles and two turtle eggs called for above—a recipe for homemade clay is on page 36.

Getting Ready
Several Days Before the Activity

If you don't have a live box turtle, borrowing one is well worth the effort. Observing, holding, and caring for a turtle is a wonderful experience for students.

Setting Up for the Turtle Drama

1. Hide the two small toy turtles under the sand in the dishpan. Put them in a place where you will be able to find them easily.
2. Put a strawberry and a piece of tomato on top of the sand.
3. Place the large toy turtle on the sand with its mouth near the strawberry.
4. Put the toy dog and the two "turtle eggs" in the paper bag.
5. Hide the container and the bag in the area where the children will watch the drama.

Getting to Know a Live Turtle

1. Sit on the floor in a circle with the students. Put the live turtle on the floor in front of you with its head facing away from you. You probably will have to hold it to keep it from escaping.

2. Tell the students they will each have an opportunity to touch the turtle's legs and shell. Ask, "Why is it best **NOT** to touch the turtle's head?" [fingers could hurt its eyes; it may bite]

3. Give each child a chance to touch the turtle. When you put the turtle on the floor, always face the head away from the child.

4. If the turtle hides in its shell, ask, "Why do you think the turtle pulls its head and legs into its shell?" Encourage the students to make suggestions.

IMPORTANT!

Turtles can carry salmonella, which causes an infection in the intestinal tract in people. Before you introduce a live turtle to the students, make sure it has been checked for salmonella and parasites. A veterinarian can do a simple test on the turtle's stool sample and let you know in a day if the turtle is safe to use. As with any animal, always make sure the children wash their hands after handling it.

Caring for a Box Turtle

Box turtles are in general very hearty and will stay that way if you follow a few simple guidelines.

The turtle's container needs to be about 2 feet by 3 feet with high enough sides so the turtle cannot climb out. It needs to have a shallow dish of water where the turtle can soak as well as drink. It should also have an area of soil where the turtle can crawl and dig, and which also helps to humidify the container. The container should have a warm and cool end so the turtle can regulate its own temperature.

The turtle needs to get a minimum of at least 10 minutes a day of direct sunlight—either that or have an UV (ultraviolet) bulb no more than 12 inches away from the turtle—so it can bask in the warmth.

Box turtles are omnivores and will eat just about anything. Dark green vegetables such as spinach are good, as are fruits such as berries and tomatoes. Canned (moist) dog food is also excellent as it contains calcium. It is a good idea to add a vitamin/mineral supplement, in addition to a calcium supplement, to the turtle's food.

The turtle needs to be washed in fresh water about once a week (no soap) and lightly rubbed all over with a vitamin A and E oil. They also need to have their beaks and nails trimmed occasionally.

Follow these steps and your box turtle should enjoy up to 20 years of life and give a great deal of pleasure to your students.

5. Point out the section on the underside of the shell that opens and closes. Explain that it is like a door with hinges.

6. Along with the children, count the turtle's eyes, legs, and toes.

7. Put the strawberry and a piece of tomato in front of the turtle to see if it will eat them.

8. Put the live turtle in its terrarium or container to keep it safe.

9. Show the Turtle Laying Eggs poster to the students. Ask,
    "What do you see in the picture?" [turtle and her eggs]
    "Where is the turtle laying her eggs?" [in the ground]

Box turtles usually lay their eggs in dirt. We substituted sand for the activity because it is a cleaner material.

Turtle Drama

Present a drama about a mother turtle laying eggs and baby turtles crawling out of their nest. Use the toys and tub of sand to act out turtle behavior as you tell the story.

- A mother turtle is eating a strawberry on a hot, sunny day.
- A dog sniffs the ground as it walks toward the turtle. What do you think a turtle would do if a dog came too close to it? (Allow time for the students to answer. If possible, place the turtle's legs, head, and tail under its shell.)
- The turtle is so still and looks so much like a rock that the dog walks away. (Walk the dog to the bag and put it away).
- The mother turtle is about to lay eggs. She needs to find a safe place to hide them.
- She uses her back legs to dig a hole in the sand and drops her eggs into the hole. (Place the two eggs in the hole.)
- She uses her back legs to cover the eggs with sand so that they are hidden.
- She then leaves her nest. (Walk the turtle to the bag and put her away).
- A long time goes by. Then something exciting happens. The baby turtles hatch out of their eggs, dig through the sand, and suddenly appear. (Crawl the turtles out from under the sand.)
- The baby turtles rest in the sun. They look for food. What do you think they will eat? [strawberries, tomatoes]
- The little turtles nibble on the strawberry and tomato. They are big enough to take care of themselves.

Creative Play

Leave the toy turtles, dog, eggs, and tub of sand out for the children to play with during their free time.

Going Further

1. Ask the class to think of other animals that lay eggs on land. The children can look through books for pictures of animals laying eggs or hatching from eggs on land. (See Resources on page 56.)

2. The series of pop-up books on page 60 in the Literature Connections complement this session. Each book highlights a particular animal (crocodile, duck, lizard, owl, penguin, or turtle), where it lays its eggs, and the parent's role in hatching the eggs.

Session 2: Eggs in Water

What You Need

For the group

❑ 1 live fish in a fish bowl
❑ 1 container of fish food
❑ 1 Fish Laying Eggs poster (see page 39)
❑ 1 bunch of pond plants
❑ 1 container, such as a basket
❑ 1 tub, such as a dishpan, filled with sand and a few dry leaves
❑ 1 tub, such as a dishpan, filled with water
❑ 10 or more hollow plastic eggs that open and close
❑ 5 or more different toy animals—small enough to fit inside the eggs—that hatch from eggs on land (such as turtles, at least one snake, snails, or crickets)
❑ 5 or more different toy animals—small enough to fit inside the eggs—that hatch from eggs in water (such as crabs, lobsters, and at least four fish)
optional
    ❑ 1 watercolor set
    ❑ 1 watercolor brush
    ❑ 1 small container of real, natural-colored salmon eggs
      (available where fishing supplies are sold)

The toy animals need to be plastic or another material that can be put in water.

Getting Ready
Anytime Before the Activity

If you don't have a goldfish in your classroom, try to borrow one and its bowl for several days. Goldfish are very easy and inexpensive pets to keep, and students enjoy watching them and taking turns feeding them.
optional
Use the watercolor set to color the poster.

Setting Up for the Baby Fish Drama

1. Put four plastic eggs (with a toy fish inside each egg) and a few pond plants in the tub of water.

2. Put the toy snake in the tub of sand and hide it under the leaves.

Getting to Know a Live Fish

1. Gather the children in a circle on the floor around the fish bowl and ask, "What is the fish doing?" [swimming] "What parts of its body does it use when it swims?" [its tail, its fins]

2. Ask, "What does a fish eat?" Let a child drop a pinch of fish food, and another child put a pond plant, into the fish bowl. Watch to see if the fish eats.

3. Show the Fish Laying Eggs poster to the group. Ask,
   "What do you see in the picture?" [fish, plants, eggs]
   "Do fish lay their eggs in the water or on land?" [in the water]
   "Where is the mother fish laying her eggs?" [on the plants in the water]

4. Tell the children that real baby fish hatch from eggs in water.

optional
   Show the real salmon eggs to the group. Let the students touch and smell the eggs.

Baby Fish Drama

1. Gather the students in a circle and present a short drama emphasizing the behavior of newly hatched fish. Place the tub of water (with plastic eggs) in the circle. Place the tub of sand (with leaves and snake) in the circle next to the tub of water so the two tubs are touching each other. Use the props to act out the drama as you tell the story.
   - Something is wiggling out of one of these eggs. What do you think it is? (Give the students time to guess. Open one egg and wiggle a fish through the water.)
   - Look! The other eggs are hatching. (Open the eggs.)
   - The baby fish swim around the pond and nibble on the pond plants.
   - A snake slithers from under the leaves and over to the pond. (Move the snake across the sand and into the water.) It goes for a swim.
   - A baby fish swims by. The hungry snake sees the fish and wants to eat it. The snake swims around the pond chasing the fish.
   - The fish hides in the pond plants and the snake swims off looking for something else to eat.
   - The fish rests in the plants after the chase and then nibbles on the plants.
   - Another fish swims around the pond. It does not see the snake swimming toward it. Snap. The snake gobbles up the fish.

2. Ask, "What did the baby fish do when they hatched out of their eggs?" [swam]

3. Ask, "What did the baby fish eat?" [pond plants] Tell the group most real baby fish can take care of themselves as soon as they hatch from their eggs. They can find their own food.

4. Ask, "What did the snake eat?" [a fish]
   "How did the fish that got away save itself?" [hid in the plants]

Creative Play

1. Create a play area where the children can continue to learn about animals that lay eggs on land and in the water. Three or four students at a time can share the materials. Set up the props from The Baby Fish Drama (tub of water, tub of sand, plastic eggs, toy fish, toy snake, and pond plant) as well as additional toy animals and eggs.
    a. In the tub of water, put the pond plant and several plastic eggs (with a toy fish or crayfish inside each egg).
    b. In the tub of sand, put four or more eggs (with a toy snake, turtle, snail, or cricket inside each egg).

2. Give the children plenty of time to play freely with the eggs, toy animals, tub of sand, and tub of water.

3. When the students finish playing, ask them to wash off the eggs and animals and spread them out to dry. Later the youngsters can put the animals in the eggs and the eggs in the basket.

This is a messy activity, best done outside. Have extra clothing or smocks for the children in case they get wet or muddy.

Going Further

Ask the class to think of other animals that lay eggs in water. The students can look through books for pictures of animals laying eggs or hatching from eggs in water. (See Resources on page 56.)

Session 3: Making Clay Eggs and Animals

What You Need
For the group
optional
   ❏ 1 plastic bag
   ❏ 1 twist-tie

For each child and yourself
   ❏ 1 ball of potter's or home-
      made clay, about the size of
      a chicken egg

Homemade Clay Recipe
This recipe provides enough clay to make eight eggs.
   ❏ 2 cups baking soda
   ❏ 1 tsp. cooking oil
   ❏ 1 cup corn starch
   ❏ 1¼ cup cold water

Soft homemade clay is usually easier for very young children to manipulate than potter's clay.

Directions

   a. Mix the baking soda, corn starch, cooking oil, and water in a pan.
   b. Cook over medium heat and stir constantly until the mixture is the consistency of mashed potatoes.
   c. Put the mixture on a plate and cover it with a damp cloth until it cools.
   d. Knead the mixture until it is smooth.

Getting Ready
Several Days Before the Activity

1. Shape the clay into balls about 3" in diameter. Make one for each child, yourself, and a few extra. For kindergartners and first graders, make the balls resemble eggs.

2. Keep the clay damp in a plastic bag if you do not use it immediately. Use a twist-tie to tightly close the bag.

Making Clay Eggs and Animals
For Preschool

1. Gather the students in a circle on the floor and show them a ball of clay.

2. Encourage preschoolers to use the clay to make eggs. Some may also make nests and animals that hatch from eggs.

For Kindergarten and First Grade

1. Hold up an egg-shaped ball of clay and say, "Let's pretend this ball of clay is an egg. What animal can you make that hatches from an egg?"

2. Allow time for the children to think about what they want to make. Give each child an "egg" and let them shape it into an animal.

Going Further

   Let the children decorate their clay eggs.
   If you do not plan to fire the clay, the students can use tempera paint to decorate them.
   If you are using potter's clay and plan to fire the clay, pound the clay and shape it carefully to avoid air pockets. Have the children glaze their clay eggs.

For Kindergarten and First Grade

   As a classroom project, encourage the students to create land and water habitats for the clay animals, nests, and eggs they make. The land habitat can include backyard soil, rocks, and possibly a small tree branch to simulate a tree for a bird nest. The students can use blue construction paper, rocks, and a small piece of driftwood for the water habitat. They can sort their clay creations by placing the land animals on land and the pond animals in "water."

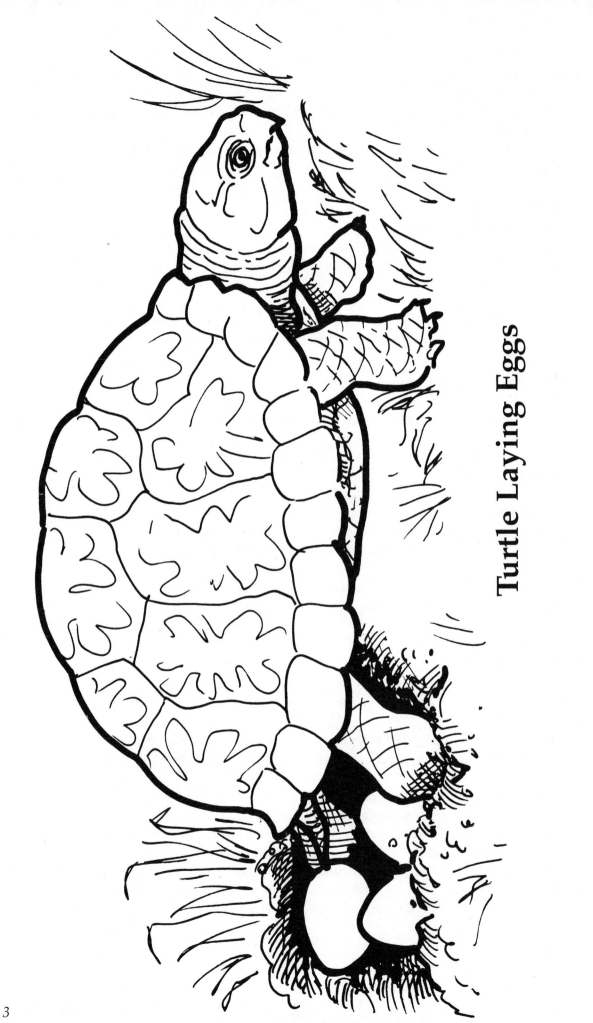

Turtle Laying Eggs

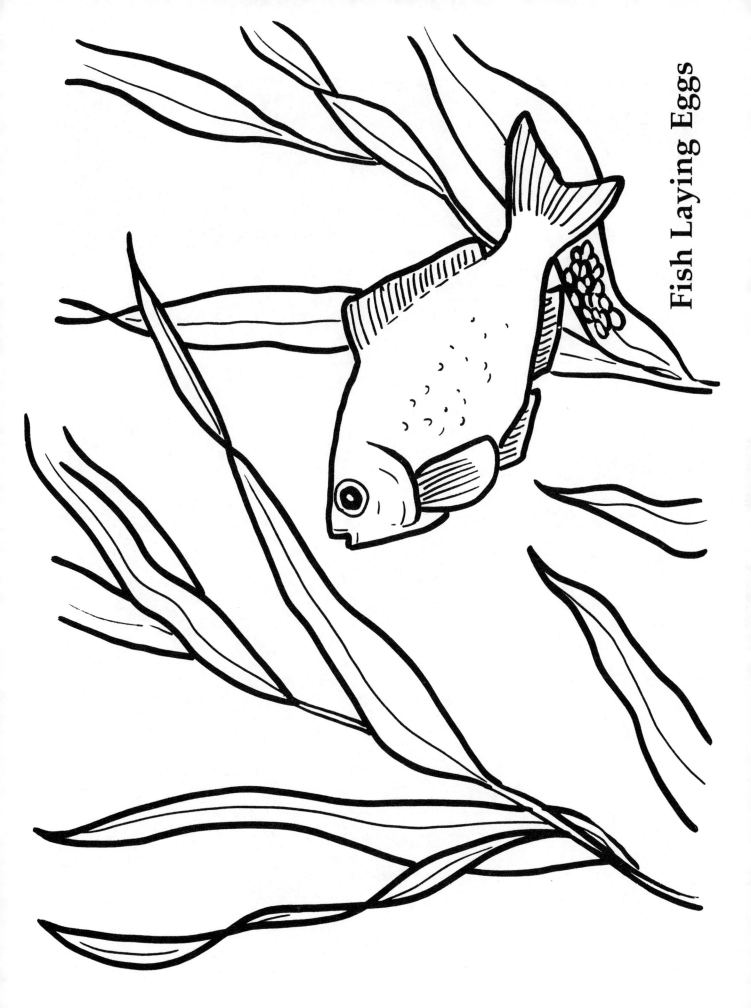

Fish Laying Eggs

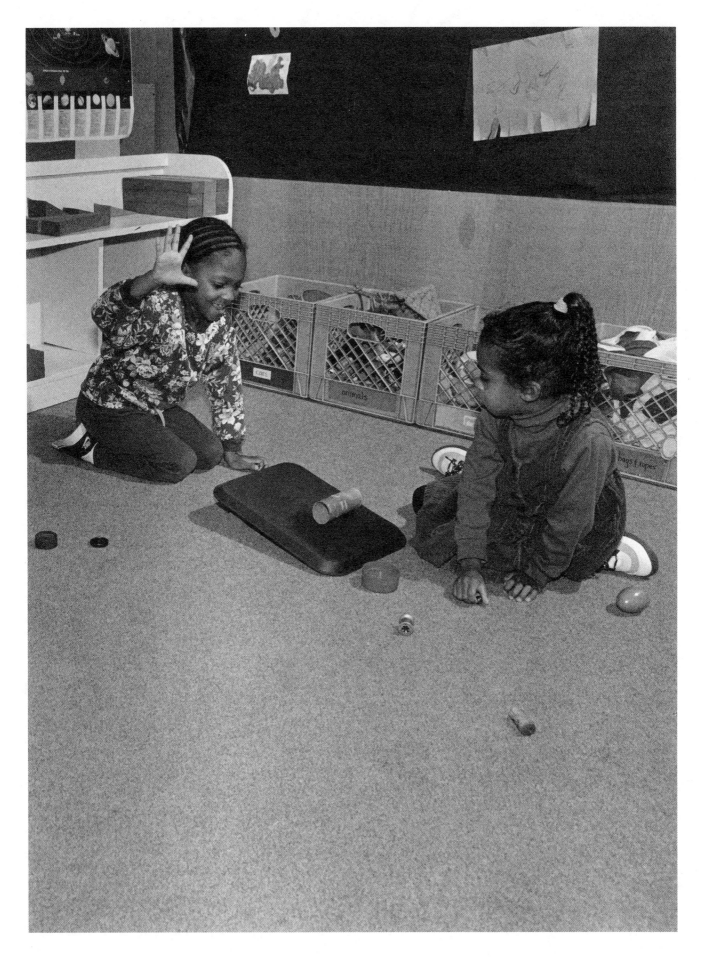

Activity 4: Rolling Eggs and Other Objects

Overview

The children freely explore the movement of plastic eggs and other objects on flat and inclined surfaces. They compare the movement of the eggs with a cork, a pinecone, a spool, and a variety of other objects as they roll them on the floor, into a box, and down a ramp. They discover eggs and balls always roll; boxes usually don't; and some objects, such as buttons, roll only if they are positioned in a certain way. They learn some objects roll faster and some roll farther than others. The children come up with their own ideas and try them out.

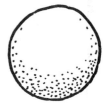

As your students freely experiment with rolling objects, they gain elements of practical experience in physical science. Some students may relate the size or shape of an object to how far and how fast it rolls. Some may verbalize their own explanation of why one ball rolls farther. Students are encouraged to experiment and test their own hypotheses.

In Session 2: Eggs on a Cliff, the children participate in a drama about a murre, a seabird that lays its egg on a narrow cliff above the ocean. The wind, the rain, and the movements of the parent bird cause the egg to roll, but it usually doesn't roll off the cliff. The students discover the shape of the murre's egg enables it to roll in a small circle. The students use objects found around the room that roll in a circle when they role-play seabirds on a cliff. This final activity helps the students understand that shapes in nature often serve an important function.

Session 1: Exploring Movement

What You Need
For each child
❑ 1 plastic egg

For the group
❑ Large blocks, about 3" square
❑ Small blocks, about 1" square
❑ A collection of objects that always roll, such as balls—large, small, heavy, light
❑ A collection of objects that usually don't roll, such as a small cardboard box
❑ A collection of objects that sometimes roll, such as an empty spool, a button, a cork, a plastic cup, a paper tube, and a pinecone
❑ A collection of objects that roll in a circle, such as a Styrofoam cone, plastic funnel, plastic cup, or a plastic toy pear
❑ Containers to hold the objects
❑ Several cardboard boxes, about 12" square
❑ Several cookie sheets, cafeteria trays, or other flat surfaces that can be inclined

Getting Ready

1. Cut the bottom and a side off the boxes so objects can roll into them.

2. Put the plastic eggs, blocks, balls, small boxes, spools, buttons, corks, cups, tubes, and pinecones in the container.

3. During the following activities the children often become active and noisy. Therefore, plan to do the activities with groups of four students. If necessary, schedule adult volunteers to help you.

Rolling Eggs on the Floor

1. Gather four students together on the floor. Hold up a plastic egg and ask, "What do you think will happen if someone gives this egg a push?" [it would roll, move, spin, wobble]

2. Ask for two volunteers to try rolling eggs. Have the children roll them on the floor toward a wall. If a child begins to throw an egg, show the group how to roll one.
    a. Put the egg on the floor.
    b. Give it a gentle push so that it rolls slowly toward a wall.

3. Ask questions to encourage observations.
    "How did the eggs move?"
    "Which egg rolled farther?"
    "Did the eggs roll straight or did they curve?"

4. Have the students practice rolling the eggs.

Rolling Other Objects on the Floor

1. Introduce the other materials by putting them on the floor. Encourage the students to find items that roll across the room.

2. Allow plenty of time for the students to freely explore the materials.

3. Ask questions to encourage the children to compare the eggs with the other objects.
    "Which things roll like an egg?"
    "Which rolls farther, the ball or the egg?"
    "Which rolls faster, the ball or the egg?"
    "Which things didn't roll?"

Rolling Objects into a Box

1. After the group has rolled objects for a while, introduce the boxes.

2. Put a box on the floor near each group and suggest to the students they find something that would roll into the box.

3. Once again, allow time for the students to experiment with the materials and find their own solutions to problems that arise. For example, the cork may always roll to the left of the box and never roll inside. By moving the box slightly to the left, a child may discover the cork can roll into the box. A child may want to predict the path of a rolling object and catch the object in the box.

Rolling Objects Down a Ramp

1. When the group seems ready for a new challenge, introduce a ramp. Prop up the cookie sheet on large blocks to create a ramp, and watch how the children play with it. The group may decide to roll two or more objects down the ramp at the same time to see which one goes farther. One child may decide to roll the objects while another children catches them. A child may put the box near the bottom of the ramp or across the room to see if an egg can roll down the ramp and into the box.

2. The students may use the two small blocks, a small and a large block, or only one block to prop up the cookie sheet. They may even decide to place a cork and a spool under the cookie sheet and roll the sheet around the room. Let the children come up with their own imaginative ideas and try them out.

3. If the group doesn't come up with many ideas, ask a few questions.
    "What do you think would happen if you put the box near the bottom of the ramp?"
    "What might happen if you put the cookie sheet on top of the balls?"

4. Give the students plenty of time to try these ideas. They are likely to think of new explorations by themselves.

Sharing Discoveries

Gather the group in a circle on the floor, and ask questions to encourage the students to share their discoveries. From your observations of what interested the children, select some of the following questions.

"What objects did you find that rolled?"
"What shapes were the ones that rolled?"
"Which one rolled the farthest?"
"Which one rolled the fastest?"
"Which ones didn't roll?"
"Which object made a circle when it rolled?"
"Which objects rolled into the box?"
"Did any of the objects make noises when they rolled?"
"Which ones made noises?"
"What happened when you rolled something down the ramp?"
"How did the box (or cork) move?"

Sorting and Graphing

1. Have the students sort the objects into a group of things that roll, a group of things that do not roll, and a group of things that sometimes roll. Let the students suggest other ways to sort the objects. They can sort the *distance* objects roll (which roll the farthest, which the shortest), and *how fast* objects roll (which roll fast, which roll slow).

2. With kindergarten and first grade students, you can make a bar graph of one of the sorts.

Session 2: Eggs on a Cliff

What You Need
For the group
❏ 1 Murre and Her Egg poster (see page 47)
❏ 1 pear-shaped murre "egg" about 3" long, such as a Styrofoam cone, or you can make a clay egg
❏ 1 black marker, or a peel-and-stick dot
❏ 1 paper bag large enough to hold the objects the children use for eggs
optional
  ❏ 1 white sheet
  ❏ 1 blue sheet, bath towel, or rug
  ❏ Several plastic fish

For each child
❏ 1 object that is larger at one end than the other (one that will roll in a circle), such as a Styrofoam cone, plastic or paper cup, yogurt container, plastic pear, or a funnel (Have other objects available that are not shaped like a murre egg, such as a paper roll or wooden block.)

Getting Ready
Several Days Before the Activity
If you decide to make a clay egg, shape it so it is pointed at one end and pivots in a small circle. (See the drawing of a murre egg on page 46.)

Immediately Before the Activity
1. Place enough objects that roll in a large circle around the room so each child will be able to find one. Also place a number of objects that do not roll.

Setting Up for the Seabird Drama
1. You can use your hand as a "bird." Your four fingers held close together are the upper bill and your thumb is the lower bill. Use a black marker to draw an eye on the bird, or use a peel-and-stick dot.

2. Use the table or counter as a "cliff." Make sure there is enough room in front of the cliff for your class to see the drama.

3. Prop up the Murre and Her Egg poster on the cliff, or tape it to the wall above the cliff.

4. Place the large pear-shaped "egg" on the table or counter.

optional
> To make the drama more visual, create an ocean cliff scene.
> a. Drape the white sheet over the table or counter to make a cliff. Place the egg on the sheet. Smooth out the sheet so the egg can roll.
> b. To create the ocean, place the blue sheet, towel, or rug on the floor in front of the cliff. Scatter several plastic fish in the ocean.

The Seabird Drama
1. Gather the students around the table. Tell them to pretend the table is a cliff and your hand is a bird called a murre, which lays its egg on a high cliff next to the ocean.

2. Ask, "How many eggs do you see on the cliff?" [one] Tell the class that a murre lays only one egg.

3. Present a drama emphasizing the egg.
   - The murre dives into the ocean to catch a fish to eat. (Move your hand down to the ocean and pretend the bird is eating a fish.)
   - The mother bird flies up to the cliff and checks her egg. (Move your hand up to the egg. Touch it gently to make it roll.)
   - Ask, "What is happening to the egg?" [it's rolling around in a circle]
   - A strong wind picks up and blows the egg. (Have a child pretend to be the wind and gently roll the egg.)
   - Ask, "Why do you think the egg rolls in a circle?" [the shape] (Encourage students to come up with their own explanations.)
   - Ask, "What would happen if the egg rolled in a straight line and fell off the cliff?" [it would break]

Find a Murre Egg

1. Tell the children that they are going to role-play mother and father murres, but first they each need to find a pretend egg, which can be any small object that rolls in a circle.

2. Have the children look around the room for pretend murre eggs.

Role-Playing Mother and Father Murres

1. When the students each have an "egg," encourage them to pretend they are either murres caring for their eggs or the wind blowing the eggs.

2. After the role-play, tell the class to place their eggs in the paper bag so later they can try rolling the different objects.

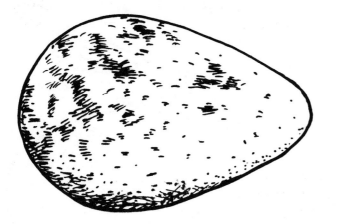

The Murre's Egg
Eggs eggs on the ground
In a circle roll around
Won't fall off the cliff we think
Will circle backwards
From that brink
Will survive, so we've heard
To hatch into a murre bird.
— *Lincoln Bergman*

Going Further

1. Give the students a sheet of paper with a drawing of a murre egg on it. Have them color it as they wish. Explain that murre eggs come in many colors and have many patterns so the parent bird can recognize their own egg. After the children have colored their egg, have them cut the eggs out, mix them up, and find the egg they colored—just like a mother or father murre finds its egg.

2. Encourage the students to pretend they are eggs and roll on the floor or down a hill.

3. Make large cardboard tunnels out of boxes and let the children roll inside them.

4. Let the students design an obstacle course of ramps, tunnels, and blocks to roll their objects through.

5. Kindergartners and first graders can make a class book. Have them dictate or write about how their favorite object rolled on the floor, into the box, or down the ramp. They can also draw the object rolling.

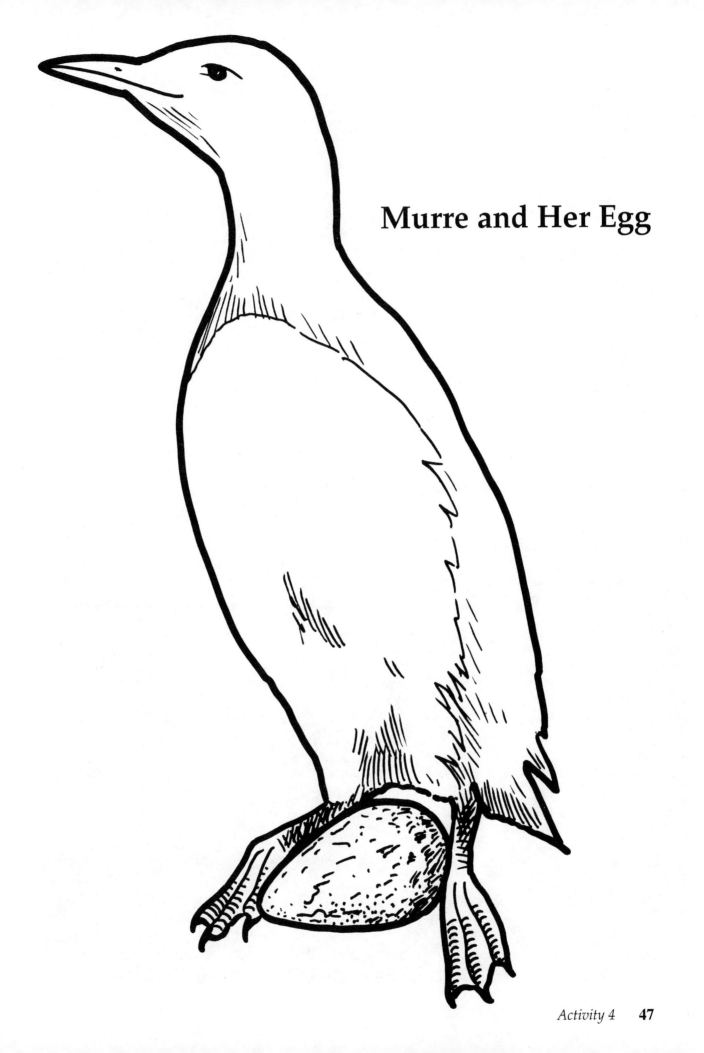

Murre and Her Egg

Background Information

Eggs are everywhere, hidden in the ground, floating in water, in beautifully constructed nests in trees, and in our houses. An interest in eggs hatches curiosity about the natural world. Why are eggs different shapes, sizes, and colors? Do all eggs have shells? Which eggs are fertilized? Which animals care for their eggs and young?

Some of the questions enthusiastic teachers, students, and parents ask most often are addressed here.

This section is for your information and use, and is not meant to be read aloud to your students.

Information about eggs and animals varies from author to author. The following is a synthesis of information researched from many sources. When reading this material, remember that whenever you generalize about animals, there are always exceptions.

Which Animals Lay Eggs?

Insects, amphibians, and birds lay eggs, as do most reptiles and fish. However, some lizards, snakes, and fish are live-bearing, meaning the female provides protection and warmth for her eggs by keeping them inside her body. When the eggs hatch, the young emerge from the female. Some species of lizards and snakes are both live-bearing and egg-laying. For example, the African chameleon (a lizard) is live-bearing in the northern part of its range. In the southern part where the climate is warmer, the chameleon lays eggs.

With mammals, the embryo grows inside the female and she gives birth to the young animal. Two notable exceptions exist—the platypus and spiny anteater, which both lay eggs.

How Many Eggs Do Animals Lay?

The number of eggs an animal lays usually depends on the young's chance of survival. The emperor penguin lays only one egg and cares for the egg and chick until the young penguin is capable of surviving on its own. In contrast, the eggs and young of most fish, amphibians, and insects usually don't have parental protection and face many more hazards—their survival depends on the production of large numbers of eggs so that at least a few of the young live to reproduce the next generation. Most fish and amphibians lay thousands of eggs. Some insects lay even more. The queen termite can lay 10,000 or more eggs in a day and up to 500 million eggs in a lifetime.

The number of eggs reptiles and birds lay varies depending on the species and the individual. Lizards typically lay one to 28 eggs. Alligators, snakes, and turtles have a greater range in the number of eggs they lay. American alligators can lay 15-88 eggs. The Indian python may lay over 100 eggs at one time, although the majority of snakes typically lay from two to 30. A box turtle may lay two to eight eggs and a sea turtle up to 200. Hummingbirds usually lay two eggs, and an ostrich lays about five eggs. (Ostriches place their eggs in a common nest, which can contain up to 21 eggs. The nest is cared for by a dominant pair of ostriches—a female and a male.)

Where Do Animals Lay Their Eggs?

Eggs are laid under the ground, on the ground, in trees, on the leaves of plants, on rocky cliffs, in the water—basically, everywhere.

Under and On the Ground

Most ants, worms, land snails, and crickets lay their eggs underground. Reptiles usually lay eggs in soil, rotting logs, and sand. Nests range from a scratch in the ground to a deep hole made by some turtles. The American alligator builds a high mound of leaves, twigs, and shrubbery and buries its eggs inside. Some species of birds, such as quail, ducks, and ostriches, lay their eggs on the ground. Their nests are often grass- or down-lined on grassland, marsh, or prairie.

In Trees

Tree holes, branches, bark, and leaves provide excellent places for animals to lay eggs. Owls, bluebirds, and some other species of birds make their nests in tree holes, as do wild honeybees. Robins and many other birds construct nests on branches. Some spiders and insects lay their eggs under bark and in tiny crevices in the bark. Some insects, including ladybugs and butterflies, lay their eggs on leaves of trees, shrubs, vegetable plants, and flowers. The leaves provide a good source of food for the young when they hatch.

On Cliffs

The common murre, the seabird featured in Activity 4 (page 44), lays its one egg on the ledge of a cliff near the ocean. It uses no nesting materials, although the parents take turns holding the egg on their feet. Eagles, sea gulls, terns, and ospreys often make large nests of sticks lined with grass and moss on cliff ledges.

In Water

Most fish, frogs, toads, and salamanders lay their eggs in water (which can range from a pond to a drop of water on a leaf), although some salamanders lay eggs in moist places, such as under logs and rocks, and in burrows. Aquatic snails and crayfish are among the many other animals that lay their eggs in water. After laying her eggs, and as a way to protect them, the female crayfish carries the eggs under her tail. Some insects, such as dragonflies and mosquitoes, also lay their eggs in water.

Why Are Eggshells Different Colors?

The coloration of eggs sometimes depends on where the eggs are laid. Speckles camouflage eggs laid on the ground. Some eggs laid on leaves are green, and some brightly colored insect eggs are often hidden under leaves.

Some birds, such as owls, which nest in dark tree holes, and turtles and crocodiles, which bury their eggs underground, have no need for camouflage. The eggs are well-hidden from predators. These eggs are often light-colored or white. The white eggs of the owl help it locate its eggs in the dark.

Common murres usually nest in crowded colonies and need to recognize their own egg from the eggs of other murres. Therefore each egg is different, varying in color and pattern. The colors range from white, cream, buff, brown, reddish, blue or green, and are marked in shades of brown or black with dots, spots, blotches, or lines.

Why Are Eggs Different Shapes?

The egg shape, whether it is round, oval, or pear-shaped, provides easy passage from the female's body. Birds with a large pelvis lay rounded eggs, those with narrow hips lay more elongated eggs. The shape also makes it easier for birds, and some other animals, to turn their eggs, which they do while incubating them to keep the embryo inside warm. Birds often turn their eggs a dozen times an hour.

The pear-shaped egg, laid by the common murre, auks, and sandpipers, among others, pivots in a small circle. This shape makes the egg less apt to roll from where it was laid.

Why Are Eggs Different Sizes?

Egg size usually depends on the size of the animal that lays it. Among birds, hummingbirds lay the smallest eggs and ostriches the largest. When birds are the same size, the ones that can run and feed themselves shortly after hatching (precocial birds—quails and ducks) lay larger eggs than birds that are helpless, blind, and usually naked after hatching (altricial birds—robins, sparrows, hummingbirds). Precocial birds develop more in the egg, thus require a larger egg.

Which Eggs Have Hard Shells and Which Don't?

Eggs have a covering to protect the growing embryo inside. Bird eggs have a hard shell, such as the shell of a chicken egg. Reptile eggshells are usually soft and rubbery. Insect eggs usually have a strong outer covering that withstands freezing weather. Amphibian eggs have a jellylike substance surrounding the egg.

Which Eggs Are Fertilized?

Most eggs that develop into embryos are fertilized, either internally or externally. Fertilization occurs when the egg fuses with the male sperm. The eggs and sperm of most fish and amphibians are fertilized externally when the eggs and sperm are deposited separately and mix, usually in water. Eggs are at risk from predators. Changes in water temperature can have destructive effects on both eggs and sperm, and they also can be destroyed if they wash ashore or the water dries up. The internal fertilization of birds and reptiles provides more protection and assures a greater chance that an embryo will develop.

In some animals, such as bees, ants, and green turtles, the sperm is stored inside the female's body for years and continues to fertilize the eggs. The honeybee queen is capable of producing young from unfertilized eggs. Male honeybees develop from unfertilized eggs and females (workers and queens) from fertilized eggs. There are also two species of lizards and the common black wasp that grow from unfertilized eggs.

What Happens Inside An Egg?

Inside many eggs, the embryo needs constant warmth in order to develop. It grows rapidly, using the yolk and some of the white for nourishment. The skeleton of the growing embryo absorbs calcium from the shell, which weakens the shell and makes it easier for the baby animal to break out. A day or two before hatching, a chick starts breathing by taking oxygen from the air chambers inside the eggshell and through the porous shell. Most unborn birds, as well as snakes, lizards, and turtles, have an "egg tooth" (a growth on the tip of the bill or upper mandible) that they use to chip at the shell. The egg tooth disappears soon after hatching. A day or so before hatching, to alert the female that hatching time is near, young birds peep faintly and young crocodiles make noise. The hatching process for birds takes from several minutes in small song birds to one or two days in some larger species. For reptiles, it takes from several hours to several days.

Which Animals Take Care of Their Eggs and Young?

Most birds brood their eggs and young, making sure they are kept warm and safe. Although this behavior is not typical of reptiles, some snakes and lizards also brood their eggs. Some reptiles, such as rattlesnakes, turn their eggs and fight off predators. Alligators guard their nests and care for their young. Most fish and amphibians lay their eggs and then leave them. Some fish guard their eggs and young until the fry (baby fish) can protect themselves. Male sea horses and pipefish protect their eggs and young by carrying them in a pouch, and some fish and frogs hold the young in their mouth when danger approaches. Honeybees, ants, and some spiders also care for their eggs and young.

Cultural Connections of Eggs

From early times, the egg has played an important role in cultures worldwide. The egg represents the miracle of new life and, as such, is both revered and mystical. In many creation myths, the egg is central. Myths from China, Egypt, Finland, and India credit the egg with the creation of the world. In North America, the Navajos believed that one of their most sacred figures, the Great Coyote Who Formed in the Water, hatched from an egg. There are many other "cosmic egg" myths and legends from early cultures, such as those from the Hindus and Incas, that tell of divinities and heroes hatching from eggs. In the Middle Ages, it was believed the earth was an egg with the yolk being the embryo where earth's metals grew.

In addition to their role in mythology, eggs were used for magical rites—some of which are still practiced today. Eggs were believed to protect against evil spirits, sickness and death, accidents, and other assorted misfortunes. In Bombay, eggs are still sometimes added to the foundations of new buildings for protection.

From Mexico comes the lively tradition of cracking confetti-filled eggs known as *cáscaras* ("eggshells") on people's heads. This ritual is part of children's birthday celebrations with everyone joining in on the fun.

Decorating Eggs

The tradition of attributing symbolic meaning to the unadorned egg has been handed down and developed to include the decorative egg as an art form.

The ancient Persians were the first people known to exchange eggs dyed in festive colors. (They did it in conjunction with the spring equinox, which marked their new year.) Clay eggs have been found in prehistoric tombs in Russia and Sweden. Eastern European countries have decorated eggs to bring luck and ward off evil since pre-Christian times. Macedonia was the first country to merge the egg-decorating tradition with the celebration of Easter. Egg traditions have continued to evolve and include fashioning eggs out of chocolate, paper, sugar, and even satin. These traditions continue to be passed down through the generations.

Red Eggs

Dyed red eggs in many cultures were believed to possess especially potent powers, and were often used as instruments to grant desires for good health, life, and fertility. In France, red eggs were offered to insure a good harvest. There is a Chinese tradition of parents giving red eggs to family and friends when their child reaches one month to celebrate the baby's survival. An older Chinese tradition was to offer red eggs to the god and goddess of the bed who, in turn, prevented babies from rolling out of the bed.

Pysanky

Dating back to before the Christian holiday of Easter, Ukrainians developed and practiced the wax-resist batik method of decorating eggs known as Pysanky ("to write" in Ukrainian). These brilliantly colored eggs are laden with meaning. The colors, motifs, and symbols that adorn them—such as stalks of wheat, flowers, leaves, and animals—recall the agricultural bounty of the Ukraine's fertile plains. The egg itself is a symbol of the annual celebration of renewal and rebirth. Pysanky eggs are meant to be kept and cherished—it is believed bowls full of these decorated eggs can keep sickness away.

What Are Your Egg Traditions?

This is by no means an exhaustive list of the egg traditions worldwide! We are still seeking traditions from around the world, and would welcome hearing about any other unique traditions that revolve around eggs. Please send GEMS your egg tradition!

Assessment Suggestions

Selected Student Outcomes

1. Students gain understanding of the role of eggs in the life cycle process.
2. Students increase their knowledge of the diversity of eggs and the wide variety of animals that hatch from them.
3. Students are able to identify selected physical characteristics of animals, and to sort and graph animals according to those characteristics.
4. Students are able to describe parenting strategies and other behaviors of animals that lay eggs on land or in water.
5. Students gain experience with the physical properties and rolling abilities of three-dimensional objects.

Built-In Assessment Activities

Eggs All Around

In Activity 1: Exploring Eggs, students are introduced to eggs, what they are, and what hatches from them through storytelling, dramatic play, visuals, and exploration of real eggs. The teacher observes how students participate in activities and discussions.
(Outcomes 1, 2)

What's Inside?

In Activity 2: Hatching Eggs, students continue to identify animals that hatch from eggs, note their physical characteristics by listening to a story, and explore toy eggs and animals. Students sort and graph the animals into groups using attributes of the various animals. The teacher can assess the students responses to questions, and involvement in the activities, to gain information on the students understanding of the sorting and graphing process.
(Outcomes 2, 3)

Wet and Dry Eggs

In Activity 3: Eggs on Land, Eggs in Water, students participate in a drama that introduces the behaviors of a box turtle and fish that lay their eggs in different places. During these activities, the teacher listens for descriptive language, explanations, responses, and questions as students compare two different parenting strategies.
(Outcomes 2, 3, 4)

Rollers and Sliders

In Activity 4, Session 1: Exploring Movement, students use plastic eggs and other three-dimensional objects to explore and compare the rolling movement of the objects on flat and inclined surfaces. As students design and conduct investigations, the teacher can observe the process and note the discussions and questions generated during the students' conversations.
(Outcome 5)

Additional Assessment Ideas

More About Eggs

Students can write and dictate stories or create an "Eggs Eggs Everywhere Book" about other animals that hatch from eggs.
(Outcomes 1, 2, 4)

Sorts and Graphs

Collect different toy animals or other objects for students to observe, sort, and graph.
(Outcome 3)

Dramatic Play

Create a play area with puppets, toy eggs, props, sorting trays, and graphs for free play and dramatic play.
(Outcomes 1, 2, 3, 4)

Rolling on

Challenge students to bring in other rolling and non-rolling items to investigate and compare.
(Outcome 5)

Resources

All About Eggs, Millicent Selsam, Addison-Wesley Publishing Co., Reading, Massachusetts, 1980.

The Amazing Egg Book, Margaret Griffin and Deborah Seed, Addison-Wesley Publishing Co., Reading, Massachusetts, 1990.

Birds' Nest, Barrie Watts, Silver Burdett, Morristown, New Jersey, 1986.

Chicken and egg, Christine Back and Jens Olesen, Silver Burdett, Morristown, New Jersey, 1982.

The Chicken and the Egg, Oxford Scientific Films, G. P. Putnam's Sons, New York, 1979.

Decorative Eggs, Candace Ord Manroe, Crescent Books, New York, 1992.

Egg, Robert Burton, Dorling Kindersley, New York, 1994.

The Egg, Gallimard Jeunesse and Pascale de Bourgoing, Scholastic, New York, 1992.

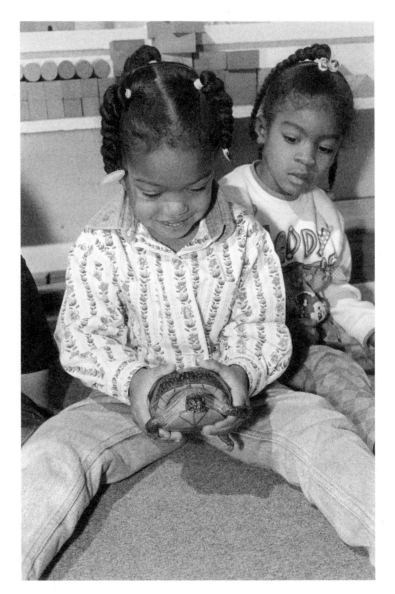

Egg! A Dozen Eggs. What Will They Be?, A. J. Wood, Little, Brown and Co., Boston, 1993.

Egg Story, Anca Hariton, Dutton Children's Books, New York, 1992.

If You Were A Bird, S. J. Calder, Silver Press, Englewood Cliffs, New Jersey, 1989.

If You Were A Fish, S. J. Calder, Silver Press, Englewood Cliffs, New Jersey, 1989.

The Little Duck, Judy Dunn, Random House, New York, 1976.

See How They Grow Series

> *Chick*, Jane Burton, Lodestar Books, New York, 1991.
>
> *Duck*, Barrie Watts, Lodestar Books, New York, 1991.
>
> *Frog*, Kim Taylor and Jane Burton, Lodestar Books, New York, 1991.
>
> *Owl*, Kim Taylor, Dorling Kindersley, New York, 1992.
>
> *Penguin*, Neil Fletcher, Dorling Kindersley, New York, 1993.
>
> *Snakes*, Kate Petty, Franklin Watts, New York, 1984.

The Turtle, Animal World Books, Troll Communications, Mahwah, New Jersey, 1988.

Turtles and Tortoises, Fred Johnson, National Wildlife Federation, Washington, D.C., 1973.

What Comes Out of an Egg?, Ernest Prescott, Watts, New York, 1976.

What's Hatching Out of that Egg?, Patricia Lauber, Crown, New York, 1979.

What's Inside? The story of an egg that hatched, May Garelick, Scholastic Book Services, New York, 1968.

Who's Hatching Here?, Alma Flor Ada, Santillana Publishing Co., Northvale, New Jersey, 1989. Available in Spanish as *¿Quien nacera aqui?*

Whose Eggs Are These?, Brian and Jillian Cutting, The Wright Group, Bothell, Washington, 1996.

Resource Materials

Hollow (blown-out) eggs

A variety of real bird eggshells (goose, finch, quail, ostrich, emu, duck, turkey, swan, and others) are available from:

> Eggs By Byrd
> Route 2, Box 2030
> Wappapello, MO 63966
> (800) 235-EGGS
> fax: (573) 222-8009

During December through March some eggs (such as quail, turkey, duck, and swan) are more difficult to get, but others (such as rhea, ostrich, emu, and goose) are still available.

Emu, ostrich, rhea, and sometimes parrot and cockatiel eggshells are available from:

Timberlake Farms
902 Ford Valley Road
Glencoe, AL 35905
(205) 492-3930

Ostrich, rhea, emu, and turkey eggshells are available from:
The Bone Room
1569 Solano Avenue
Berkeley, CA 94707
(510) 526-5252

Live (fertile) eggs, Incubators

Live insect and frog eggs, incubators (these usually include instructions), and other useful science materials are available from:
Insect Lore
P.O. Box 1535
Shafter, CA 93263
800-LIVE BUG

A variety of live eggs, incubators (these usually include instructions), and other useful science materials are available from:

Carolina Biological Supply
2700 York Road
Burlington, NC 27215
(800) 334-5551
fax: (800) 222-7112

Ward's
P.O. Box 92912
Rochester, NY 14692-9012
(800) 962-2660
fax: (800) 635-8439

Flinn Scientific
P.O. Box 219
Batavia, IL 60510-0219
(800) 452-1261
fax: (630) 879-6962

Frey Scientific
100 Paragon Parkway
P.O. Box 8101
Mansfield, OH 44901-8101
(800) 225-FREY
fax: (419) 589-1522

Murry McMurry Hatchery
191 Closz Drive
Webster City, Iowa 50595
(800) 456-3280
fax: (515) 832-2213

Sargent Welch
911 Commerce Court
Buffalo Grove, IL 60089-2375
(800) SARGENT (727-4368)
fax: (800) 676-2540

Literature Connections

Box Turtle at Long Pond
by William T. George; illustrated by Lindsay Barrett George
Greenwillow Books, New York. 1989
Grades: Preschool–2

> The events of a day for a box turtle are described
> in this nicely illustrated book.
> *Connection: Activity 3*

The Button Box
by Margarette S. Reid; illustrated by Sarah Chamberlain
Dutton Children's Books, New York. 1990
Grades: Preschool–2

> A young boy explores his grandmother's button box and categorizes but-
> tons by various attributes. After reading the story, students will be inspired
> to sort buttons many ways! Available in Spanish as *La Caja De Los Botones.*
> *Connection: Activity 2*

Chickens Aren't the Only Ones
by Ruth Heller
Grosset and Dunlap, New York. 1981
Grades: Preschool–2

> The brightly colored illustrations depict the diversity of all egg-laying
> animals as well as egg laying behaviors, and the sizes and shapes of eggs.
> Available in Spanish as *Las gallinas no son las unicas* (Grosset & Dunlap, New
> York. 1992).
> *Connection: Activity 2, Session 1*

The Chicken's Child
by Margaret A. Hartelius
Scholastic, New York. 1975
Grades: Preschool–2

> A hen hatches a crocodile egg in this wordless and humorous book. As the
> crocodile grows, it gets itself into all kinds of trouble. The crocodile almost
> loses its home until it saves its "mother's" life. This is a great book to
> develop language, and is clearly unrealistic enough so even the youngest
> reader will not be confused about what really hatches from a chicken egg.
> *Connection: Activity 2*

Circles, Triangles and Squares
by Tana Hoban
Macmillan, New York. 1974
Grades: Preschool–2

> The shapes of the title are examined using photographs of actual objects.
> The same author also wrote *Round and Round and Round* (Macmillan, New
> York. 1983), which also examines shapes, especially those that are round.
> *Connection: Activity 4*

Crocodile Egg Pop-Ups
Duck Egg Pop-Ups
Lizard Egg Pop-Ups
Owl Egg Pop-Ups
Penguin Egg Pop-Ups
Turtle Egg Pop-Ups
Illustrated by Bob Bampton
Golden Books/Western Publishing, New York. 1994
Grades: Preschool–2

> Each of these lovely pop-up books examines an animal, the shape of its egg, where it lays its eggs, and the parent's role in hatching the egg. The grand finale in each volume is the wonderful pop-up of the baby animal emerging from the egg.
> *Connections: Activity 1*
> *Activity 3 (Turtle Egg Pop-Ups)*

An Extraordinary Egg
by Leo Lionni
Alfred A. Knopf, New York. 1994
Grades: K–2

> Jessica the frog finds a beautiful, round, white egg that she mistakes for a stone. One of her frog friends recognizes it as a chicken's egg. When it hatches a few days later, they call the animal that emerges a chicken. The students will immediately delight in this mistake as they recognize the newborn animal as an alligator! Eventually the alligator is returned to its rightful mom with plenty of laughs along the way.
> *Connection: Activity 2*

Flap Your Wings
by P.D. Eastman
Random House, New York. 1969
Grades: K–2

> When Mr. and Mrs. Bird discover a strange egg in their nest, placed there by a boy, they decide to try to hatch it and are surprised when the hatchling turns out to be an alligator.
> *Connection: Activity 1*

The Golden Egg Book
by Margaret Wise Brown; illustrated by Leonard Weisgard
Western Publishing, Racine, Wisconsin. 1975
Grades: Preschool–1

> A little bunny who finds an egg isn't sure what will come out of it and is impatient to find out. When a duck finally hatches from the egg, the bunny is surprised and pleased to have a new friend.
> *Connection: Activity 1*

Remember, people will judge you by your actions, not your intentions. You may have a heart of gold— but so does a hard-boiled egg.

—*Unknown*

Horton Hatches the Egg

by Dr. Seuss (Theodore Geisel)
Random House, New York. 1940
Grades: Preschool–2

> When a lazy bird hatching an egg wants a vacation, she asks Horton, an elephant, to sit on her egg-—which he does through all sorts of hazards. In the end he is rewarded for doing what he said he would.
> *Connection: Activity 2*

Is It Larger? Is It Smaller?

by Tana Hoban
Greenwillow Books, New York. 1985
Grades: Preschool–2

> Readers are invited to find the smaller or smallest of two or more similar objects in each photograph. This helps children begin to focus on the attribute of large and small, which is one way of sorting a set of objects.
> *Connection: Activity 2*

Mrs. Sato's Hens

by Laura Min; illustrated by Benrei Huang
GoodYearBooks/Scott, Foresman and Co., Glenview, Illinois. 1994
Grades: Preschool–2

> A little girl visits Mrs. Sato's hens every day for a week. As the days go by, she and Mrs. Sato count the variety of eggs laid by different hens until a surprise ending on Saturday when they discover something new in the hen house! A variety of hens as well as hen eggs are illustrated. Available in Spanish as *Las gallinas de la senora Sato* (HarperCollins, New York. 1995).
> *Connection: Activity 1*

Rechenka's Eggs

by Patricia Polacco
Philomel Books, New York. 1988
Grades: K–2

> Babushka paints beautiful eggs through the cold of winter to take to the Easter festival. One day Babushka rescues an injured goose, which later has a terrible accident and breaks all of Babushka's eggs! However, the goose lays 13 marvelously colored eggs to replace the broken ones—and leaves behind a final miracle in egg form before returning to her own kind.
> *Connection: Activity 1*

Seven Eggs

by Meredith Hooper; illustrated by Terry McKenna
Harper & Row, New York. 1985
Grades: K–2

> Each day of the week an egg cracks open and out emerges a different animal. On the seventh day a surprise is hatched for all! The eggs that hatch are different shapes and sizes and presented in an inviting format.
> *Connection: Activity 1, Session 2*

> `Tis the part of a wise man to keep himself today for tomorrow, and not venture all his eggs in one basket.
>
> —*Miguel de Cervantes*
> *Don Quixote*

> Put all your eggs in one basket and—WATCH THAT BASKET.
>
> —*Mark Twain*
> *Pudd'nhead Wilson*

You may wish to examine the literature listings for the GEMS teacher's guides Animal Defenses, Buzzing A Hive, Group Solutions, Hide A Butterfly, Ladybugs, Tree Homes, Penguins And Their Young, and Terrarium Habitats in the GEMS handbook Once Upon A GEMS Guide: Connecting Young People's Literature to Great Explorations in Math and Science. Also, please see the age-appropriate listings in the science themes as well as the math strands sections in the handbook. In addition, the teacher's guides include exciting activities that would make excellent accompaniments to this guide.

Swimmy

by Leo Lionni

Alfred A. Knopf, New York. 1963

Grades: Preschool–2

A clever little black fish discovers a way for his school of little red fish to swim together and be protected from larger predators. With Swimmy as the "eye," the fish swim in formation masquerading as a big fish. Included are examples of other animals that live in the water.

Connection: Activity 3

Tap! Tap! ... the egg cracked

by Keith Faulkner; illustrated by Jonathan Lambert

Marlboro Books, New York. 1992

Grades: Preschool–2

A hen loses her egg and in her search for it, she encounters many kinds of eggs and the animals who laid them. The shape of each animal's egg is accurately shown in "lift the flap" fashion, which allows the reader to peek in and see the baby animal hatching out of its egg. Of course, mother hen finds her egg and out of it comes a sweet little chick!

Connection: Activity 1 and 2

Tracks in the Sand

by Loreen Leedy

Doubleday, New York. 1993

Grades: Preschool–3

With full-page illustrations and clear text, the life cycle of loggerhead turtles is described, beginning with the female leaving the sea to bury her eggs in the sand. An afterword provides more in-depth biological information.

Connection: Activity 3

Whose Shoes Are These?

by Ron Roy; photographs by Rosemarie Hausherr

Clarion Books/Ticknor and Fields, New York. 1988

Grades: Preschool–4

Nineteen types of shoes and footwear are depicted in photographs of children and adults from around the world. Children can examine their own shoes and sort and classify them. Also of interest, by the same author and publisher, is *Whose Hat is That?* (1987), which explores a variety of hats.

Connection: Activity 2

The Wolf's Chicken Stew

by Keiko Kasza

G. P. Putnam's Sons, New York. 1987

Grades: K–2

A hungry wolf attempts to fatten a chicken for his stew pot by bringing delectable items to the chicken's doorstep in quantities or weights of 100. When the wolf finally arrives to capture the chicken for his stew, he has quite a surprise as the hen's many little chicks come out to greet him.

Connection: Activity 1

Summary Outlines

Activity 1: Exploring Eggs
Session 1: What is an Egg?

The Chicken Drama
1. Gather the class in a circle and ask, "What is an egg?" "Has anyone ever seen a real egg?" "What kind of egg was it?" "Where did you see it?"
2. Present a short drama about Linda and her mystery eggs.
3. Show the Chicken and Her Nest poster and a toy chicken. Ask, "What do you think Linda (the doll) could do with the eggs?"
4. Ask questions to encourage discussion of past experiences with chickens.

Observing Chicken Eggs
Give a chicken egg to each child and ask questions to encourage observation and discussion.

Role-playing
1. Role-play with the children the drama of chicks hatching out of eggs.
2. Show pictures of newly hatched chicks.

Creative Play
Let the students play with the doll, toy chicken, nest, and eggs.

Session 2: A Variety of Eggs
Observing a Variety of Real Eggs
Have the children observe a variety of eggs. Encourage them to compare the size, shape, and color of the eggs.

Animal Pictures
1. Show the Snake Laying Eggs, Robin and Her Nest, and Ostrich and Her Eggs posters and ask questions about each poster.
2. Show pictures of other animals hatching from eggs or laying eggs.

Find an Egg
1. Show a plastic egg and have each child find one egg (of the several you placed outside earlier).
2. Have each child open their egg and take turns identifying the animals inside. Tell them real animals like these (name the toy animals you have) hatch from eggs.
3. Have the children place the animals back into the eggs, and leave the basket of eggs and animals out for the children to freely explore later.

Activity 2: Hatching Eggs
Session 1: Sorting Animals

Animal Sorting
1. Ask the students what animals hatch from eggs. Read *Chickens Aren't the Only Ones*.
2. Hold up a plastic egg and have the children guess what is inside. Open it and let everyone see the toy animal that "hatched" from the egg. Give each child an egg with a toy inside. Let them guess what is inside, then open their eggs.
3. Place a paper plate in the center of the circle of students. Have students with toy fish put them on the plate. Count with the students the number of fish.
4. Place a second paper plate. Have students with spiders put them on the second plate. Count with students the number of spiders.
5. Continue in this fashion until all the toy animals of the same kind are on plates and you have counted with the students the number of each type of animal.
6. Ask questions such as "How many plates have only two animals?" "How many plates have more than three animals?"
7. For older students ask questions such as, "If you put the snake and a fish together, how many animals would you have?"
8. Ask what all the animals have in common. [hatch from eggs]

Role-Playing Animals
1. Present an egg-hatching drama. Have the children curl up and pretend they are in an egg. Have them get bigger and break out of the egg and pretend to be an animal.
2. Have the other students guess in turn which animal each student is pretending to be.

Session 2: Organizing Sorts Into Graphs
For Kindergarten and First Grade Only

Animal Sorting and Graphing
1. Give each student a plastic egg with an animal inside and have them open their egg.
2. Ask which animals have legs and which have no legs.
3. Have a student place an animal with no legs on a paper plate.
4. Have a student place an animal with legs on a second paper plate.
5. Have all the students place their animals on the appropriate plate.
6. Have the students guess which is the bigger group of animals, and ask them how you can determine it. [counting]
7. Introduce Side 1 of the graphing grid.
8. Place an animal with legs in the first row, first column.
9. Place an animal without legs in the second row, first column.
10. Help the students place their animals in the appropriate rows until all the animals are placed on the grid.
11. Ask the students which group of animals (with or without legs) has the most animals.
12. Count the number of animals in each row.
13. Explain the idea of "partners" on the grid and assign the animals on the grid partners until there is a column with no partners.
14. Count the number of animals without partners. Tell the students that is how many more animals one group has than the other group.

Graph Again

1. Tell the students they are going to organize the animals by how many legs each animal has.
2. Gather the animals and give each child one animal. Have them count the number of legs on their animal.
3. Place number labels on Side 2 of the graphing grid.
4. Ask for animal with no legs and have the student place it in the "0" row. Ask for a two-legged animal and have the student place it in the "2" row. Continue in this fashion until all the animals are placed on the grid.
5. Ask questions such as "How many animals on the graph have _____ (0, 2, 4, 6, 8, 10) legs?"
6. For first grade students ask questions using the idea of fewer than.
7. Ask students addition questions such as "If we add the number of animals with two legs and the number of animals with eight legs together, how many animals would we have?"
8. Remind students what all the animals have in common. [hatch from eggs]

Activity 3: Eggs on Land, Eggs in Water
Session 1: Eggs on Land

Getting to Know a Live Turtle

1. Let the students see and touch a box turtle. Warn them not to touch its head. Ask why the turtle hides its head in its shell and point out the underside "hinge."
2. Count the turtle's legs, eyes, and toes with the students.
3. Show the Turtle Laying Eggs poster and ask questions about it.

Turtle Drama

Present the drama about a turtle laying eggs.

Creative Play

Let the children play freely with the toys, eggs, and tub of sand.

Session 2: Eggs in Water
Getting to Know a Live Fish

1. Gather the children around the fish bowl and ask questions about the fish.
2. Let one child put food into the fish bowl.
3. Show the Fish Laying Eggs poster and ask questions about it.

Baby Fish Drama

Present the Baby Fish Drama and ask questions about it afterward.

Creative Play

Let the children freely play with the drama props, the toy animals and plastic eggs.

Session 3: Making Clay Eggs and Animals
Making Clay Eggs and Animals
For Preschool

Show preschoolers the balls of clay, give each child one, and encourage them to make their own egg.

Show the students the egg-shaped balls of clay, give each child one, and encourage them to make an animal that might hatch from the clay egg.

Activity 4: Rolling Eggs and Other Objects
Session 1: Exploring Movement

Rolling Eggs on the Floor
1. Show the students a plastic egg and ask what will happen if it is pushed on the floor.
2. Have two volunteers roll an egg.
3. Ask questions about how the egg rolled. Have students practice rolling eggs.

Rolling Other Objects on the Floor
Introduce various objects and have students find items that will roll. Ask questions about how the objects rolled.

Rolling Objects into a Box
Introduce the boxes. Let students experiment with rolling objects into the boxes.

Rolling Objects Down a Ramp
Introduce a ramp. Let the students experiment with rolling objects down a ramp and any variations they wish. Ask questions, if necessary, to vary how they use the ramp.

Sharing Discoveries
Have the students share what they discovered about how the various objects rolled.

Sorting and Graphing
1. Have the students sort the objects into those that rolled, those that didn't roll, and those that sometimes rolled. Sort in other ways, such as by distance and speed.
2. Kindergarten and First Grade students can make a bar graph of one of the rolling object sorts.

Session 2: Eggs on a Cliff
The Seabird Drama
1. Gather the students around a table and tell them it is a cliff and your hand (with its black dot) is a mother murre bird. Ask how many eggs they see on the cliff. [one]
2. Present the Seabird Drama.

Find a Murre Egg
Have the children pretend they are father and mother murres. Have them look around the room for an object that rolls in a circle (which you placed earlier).

Role-Playing Mother and Father Murres
As father and mother murres, have the students care for their eggs by rolling them, or pretending to be the wind, blowing to make them roll.

Eight Egg Odes

Eggs eggs all around
Deep in sea
Or underground
Hatching into
Many things
Some with legs
Some with wings.

Eggs eggs in the nest
Which kind of egg
Do you like best?
Big as ostrich
Small as wren
From a snake
Or from a hen?

Eggs eggs sure are swell
In special skin
We call a shell
Inside the egg
Life grows and grows
When will it hatch?
Nobody knows!

Eggs eggs
Everywhere
Needing warmth
Needing care
They will hatch
When time is right
Life will leap into the light!

From garter snake
To bluejay feather
Coldest climes
To warmest weather
Spider sac
To salmon leap
Mountain high to ocean deep.

There's many sorts
Of eggs you see
They come in great diversity
They're part of
Many celebrations
And you can make
Great eggs-plorations!

Take one "e"
Add two "g"s
For a wondrous hatchery
Animals with claw and tooth
Spring forth
From eggs—
And that's the truth!

It's amazing,
That's no yolk
Eggs are loved by every folk
Baby creatures breaking free
From eggs on land and under sea
Seagulls soaring through the air
Eggs eggs everywhere!

by Lincoln Bergman

Chicken and Her Eggs

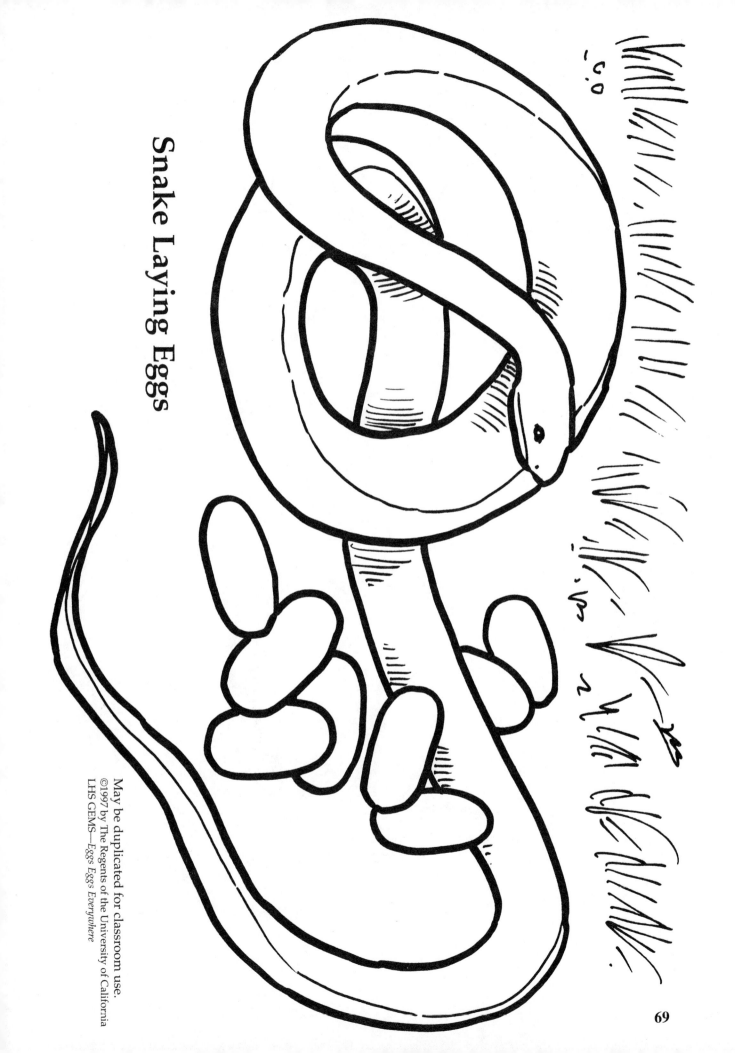

Snake Laying Eggs

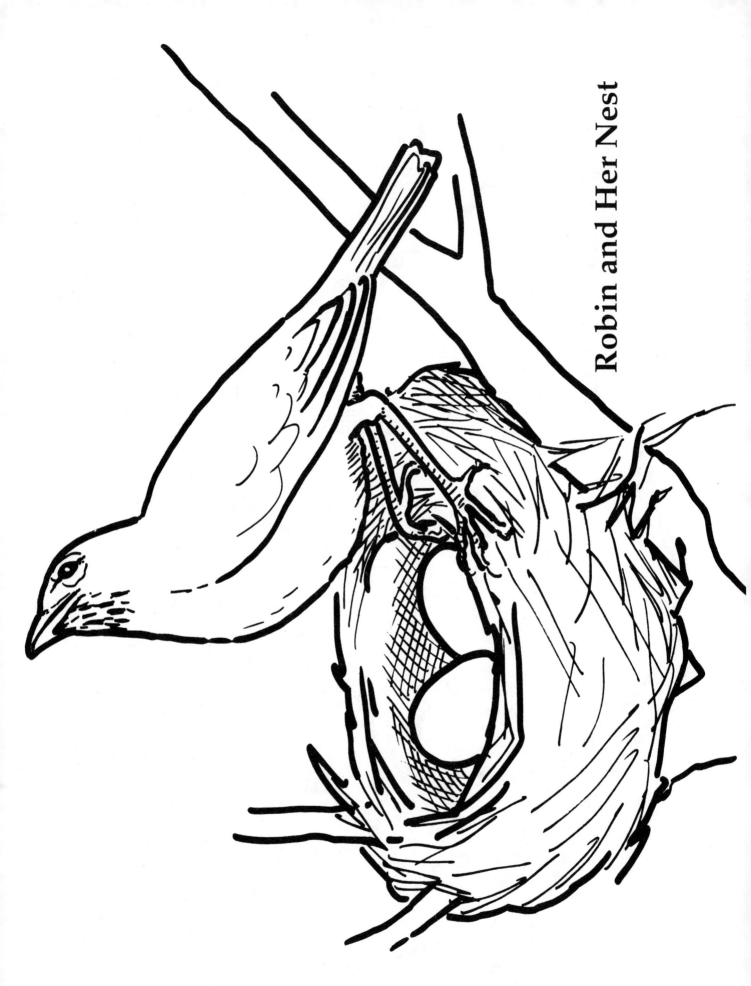

Ostrich and Her Eggs

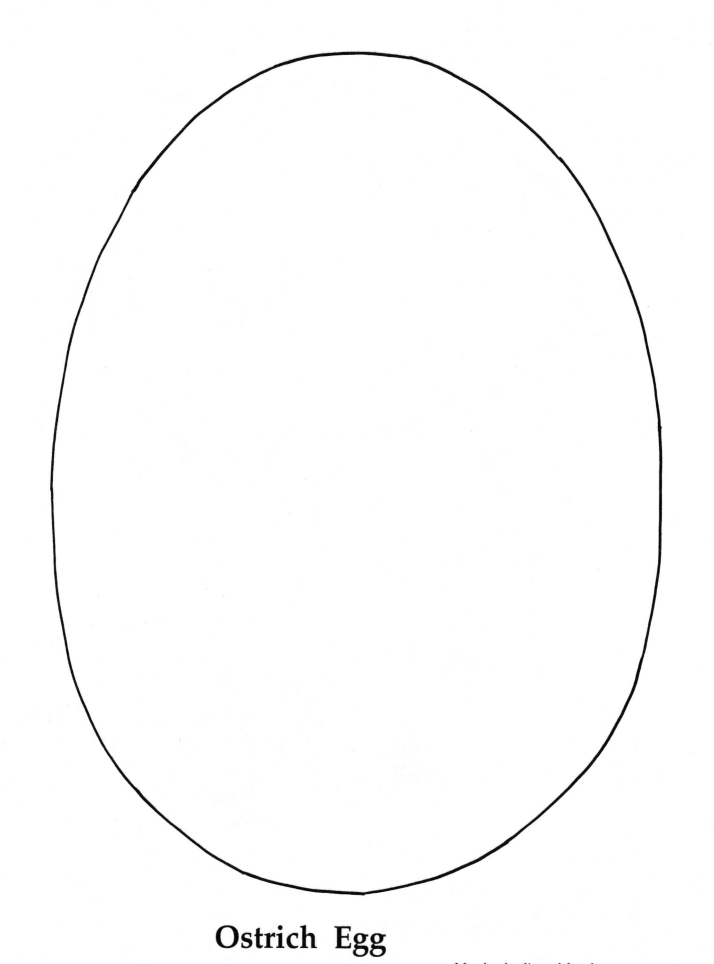

Ostrich Egg

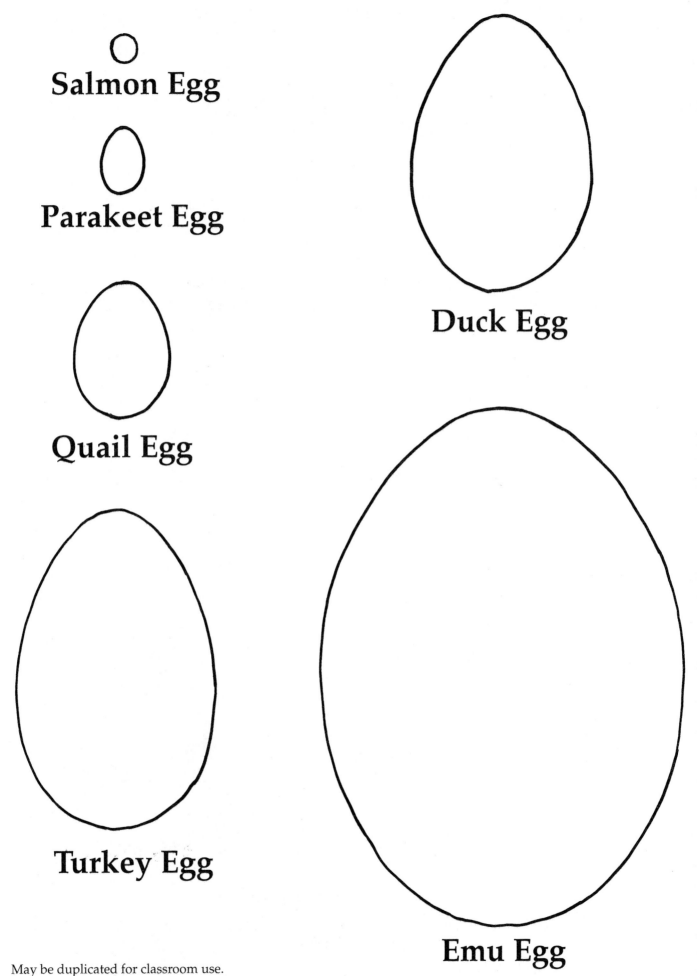

Salmon Egg

Parakeet Egg

Quail Egg

Turkey Egg

Duck Egg

Emu Egg

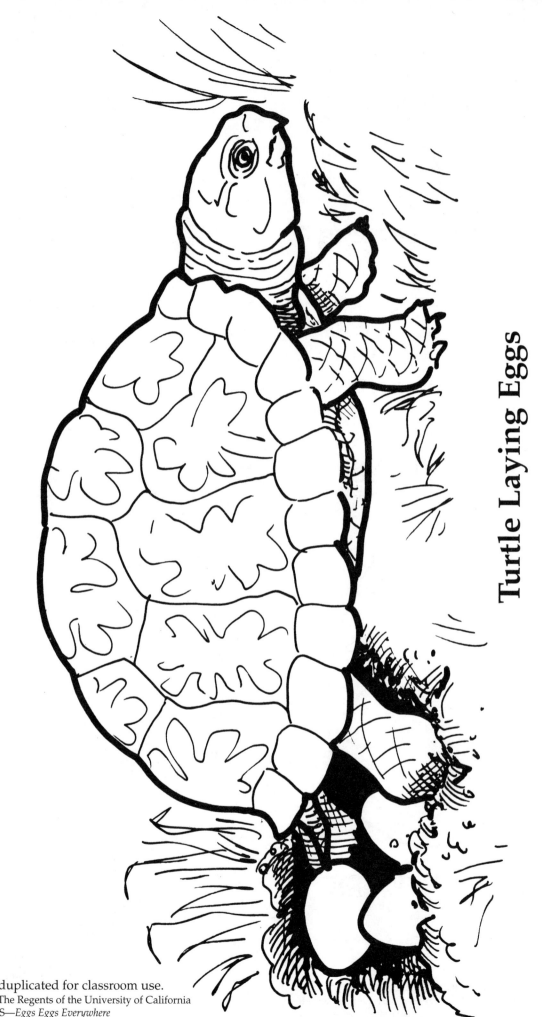

Turtle Laying Eggs

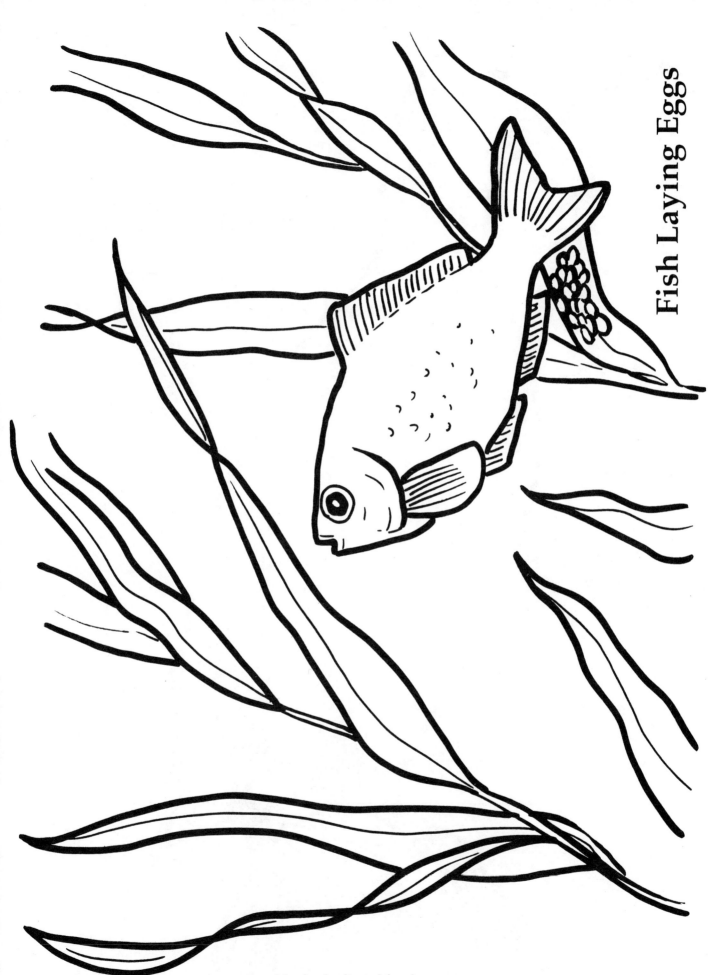

Murre and Her Egg